LAOS

TRAVEL GUIDE 2023-2024

Exploring the Heart of Southeast Asia: A Comprehensive Travel Guide to Enchanting Laos- Discover Cultural Riches, Ancient Temples, Culinary Delights, and Unforgettable Adventures.

BY

Joan A. Pearl

Copyrighted Material

Copyright © 2023 by Joan A. Pearl

All rights reserved. No part of this publication may be reproduced, distributed, or transmitted in any form or by any means, including photocopying, recording, or other electronic or mechanical methods, without the prior written permission of the publisher, except in the case of brief quotations embodied in critical reviews and certain other noncommercial uses permitted by copyright law.

MY VACATION EXPERIENCE..6
   Why You Should Visit Laos.................................. 7
   The People of Laos... 12
   The Language of Laos....................................... 16
   The Religion of Laos... 19
   The History of Laos..22

CHAPTER 1... 27
   Introduction to Laos.. 27
   What is There to See and Do in Laos?.............. 30
   When is the Best Time to Visit Laos?.............. 34
   What to pack for your trip to Laos................... 38
   Laos travel essentials..42
   Where to Stay in Laos...................................... 48
   Budgeting for Your Laos Trip........................... 52
   Getting Ready for Your Laos Trip..................... 57

CHAPTER 2... 63
   How to Choose Your Laos Itinerary................. 63
   Visas and Currency Exchange......................... 71
   Travel Insurance for Laos................................ 78
   Booking your flights and accommodation....... 84
   Health and Safety in Laos................................87

CHAPTER 3... 93
   Getting Around Laos.. 93
   Domestic Flights in Laos.................................. 93

  Buses in Laos..98
  Trains in Laos.. 101
  Boats in Laos... 105
  Taxis and Tuk-Tuks in Laos... 110
  Rental Cars in Laos...113
CHAPTER 4.. 117
  Things to Do in Laos.. 117
  Luang Prabang... 117
  Vientiane.. 122
  Vang Vieng.. 126
  Si Phan Don (Four Thousand Islands),...................... 129
  Thakhek... 132
  Pakse.. 135
  Champasak... 139
  Muang Ngoi Neua.. 143
CHAPTER 5.. 147
  Activities.. 147
  Hiking and Trekking... 147
  Kayaking and Rafting... 150
  Elephant Trekking.. 154
  Cooking Classes... 158
  Shopping... 161
  Nightlife..164

CHAPTER 6..**169**
    Food and Drinks in Laos... 169
    Lao Food..169
    Lao Drinks... 173
    Where to Eat in Laos... 176

CHAPTER 7..**181**
    Tips for Traveling in Laos... 181
    Be Prepared for the Heat and Humidity...................... 181
    Learn Some Basic Lao Phrases................................... 184
    Bargain When Shopping..187
    Be Respectful of Local Culture................................... 190
    Tipping is not expected in Laos...................................193
    Cultural etiquette in Laos.. 196
    Emergency Contacts.. 199

Conclusion..**203**
    Travel planner..204

MY VACATION EXPERIENCE

The moment I set foot in Laos, I was greeted by a warm breeze carrying the scent of exotic flowers. The brilliant colors of the busy marketplaces and the sweet smiles of the residents made me feel instantly at ease. But it was the individuals that genuinely touched my heart.

I watched the sacred ceremony of Tak Bat in the historic city of Luang Prabang, where hundreds of saffron-robed monks silently traversed the streets at daybreak, collecting alms. I was brought to tears by the sight of their humility and commitment. It was a profound reminder of the power of simplicity and faith. I visited the secluded village of Nong Khiaw, which is set among high limestone cliffs, one day. There, I met Sita, a little girl with an irrepressible smile and brilliant eyes who stole my heart. We bonded on a deep level despite the language barrier, exchanging tales and dreams. In that brief instant, I knew that the beauty of human connection is beyond words.

I couldn't help but feel a deep feeling of thankfulness for nature's wonders as I toured Laos' beautiful landscapes, from the gushing waterfalls of Kuang Si to the mysterious Plain of Jars. The sheer majesty of these views moved my spirit and reminded me of how short life is.

It was heartbreaking to leave Laos since it meant saying goodbye to a place that had become a part of me. The memories I formed and the feelings I had will be treasured for the rest of my life. Laos showed me the genuine meaning of love, compassion, and the power of a single moment, with its fascinating beauty and welcoming people.

Why You Should Visit Laos

Laos, a landlocked country in Southeast Asia, is a hidden gem just waiting to be found by adventurous travelers. Laos provides travelers with a one-of-a-kind and amazing experience, thanks to its rich cultural history, magnificent scenery, and friendly residents.

In this guide, we will look at the reasons why you should visit Laos and the delights that await you in this enthralling country.

1. Captivating Natural Beauty: Laos has a broad selection of scenery that will stun nature lovers. The country's natural attractions include the lush greenery of its rainforests, the flowing Mekong River, and the beautiful limestone karsts of Vang Vieng. Outdoor activities available to visitors include walking through virgin woods, canoeing along twisting rivers, and finding secret caverns. The breathtaking Kuang Si Waterfalls, with their multi-tiered blue pools, are a must-see, providing a cool respite from the tropical heat.

2. Tranquilly and Serenity: In contrast to its more hectic neighbors, Laos is known for its serene and relaxed attitude. The slower pace of life, along with the lack of crowds, creates a perfect environment for relaxation and reflection. This tranquility is notably apparent at the UNESCO World Heritage site of Luang Prabang.

The town's colonial architecture, quiet Buddhist temples, and daily almsgiving rituals all add to a serene spiritual ambiance.

3. Diverse Cultural Heritage: Laos has a diverse cultural tapestry that is strongly entwined with Theravada Buddhism. Temples and monasteries are fundamental to the country's identity, and examining them provides insight into the Lao people's spiritual life. Laos' architectural and theological splendor is epitomized by the famous Wat Xieng Thong in Luang Prabang and the golden stupa of Pha That Luang in Vientiane. Interacting with monks and taking part in traditional rites may give a one-of-a-kind and significant cultural experience.

4. Friendly Locals: Laotians are noted for their genuine warmth and kindness. Interacting with locals frequently results in unique interactions that provide insight into their everyday lives. Visitors will be greeted with open arms whether they are having a meal at a family-run restaurant or shopping at local markets.

The Laotian way of life is a stark reminder of the importance of simplicity and community, forming long-lasting bonds with visitors.

5. Culinary Delights: Laotian cuisine combines flavors and influences from neighboring nations. Sticky rice, a mainstay of Lao cuisine, is typically accompanied by a variety of spicy sauces and fresh veggies. From aromatic herb-infused soups to hot papaya salads, the country's food provides a variety of dishes that reflect its culture and location. Trying local street cuisine and dining at traditional markets provides a one-of-a-kind gourmet experience.

6. Genuine Handicrafts: Laos has a rich handicraft culture that reflects the ingenuity and talents of its artists. The nation is a wonderful mine of unique crafts, ranging from delicate silk weaving to hand-carved woodwork. Visitors may shop for one-of-a-kind fabrics, pottery, and silverware at local workshops and marketplaces. Supporting these craftsmen not only allows you to carry home unique gifts but also helps to preserve traditional workmanship.

7. Adventure and Exploration: Laos has a plethora of options for the adventurous traveler to experience its wilder side. Northern highland trekking reveals secret hill tribal communities and stunning scenery. The intriguing Plain of Jars in Xieng Khouang Province is an archaeological conundrum, while the Bolaven Plateau enchants with its coffee plantations and roaring waterfalls.

8. Responsible and Sustainable Tourism: Laos' low visitor numbers have helped to preserve its natural and cultural assets. To guarantee that its riches are preserved for future generations, the government is increasingly focused on responsible and sustainable tourism practices. Many tour companies and hotels are dedicated to reducing their environmental effect and assisting local communities.

In conclusion, Laos exemplifies the draw of off-the-beaten-path travel. Its untouched scenery, colorful culture, and friendly residents create an ambiance that both captivates and rejuvenates. Laos delivers a memorable vacation that exceeds the ordinary, whether it's touring historic temples, going on outdoor activities, or simply enjoying the tranquility of its surroundings. As you travel through its meandering rivers and beautiful hills, you will encounter a land that exudes authenticity and begs you to immerse yourself in its enigmatic attractions. Let's delve in and explore!

The People of Laos

Laos are noted for their warm welcome, kind attitude, and love of life. They are a varied group, with Laos home to over 40 distinct ethnic groups. Despite their differences, Lao people have a cultural and historical tie. One of the most noticeable characteristics of the Lao people is their friendliness and kindness. Laos welcomes visitors with open arms and smiles.

Lao people are always keen to share their culture and customs and are always willing to help a stranger. Laos is also noted for its compassionate demeanor. They are peaceful people who hold a high regard for nature. Laos is frequently regarded as *"slow to anger and quick to forgive."* Lao people like celebrating life. They are always up for a good time and like spending time with their family and friends. Lao festivals are a veritable explosion of color, music, and dancing. If you plan a vacation to Laos, expect to be greeted with open arms. Lao people are among the world's kindest and most hospitable people. You'll have a great experience getting to know them and learning about their culture.

Here are some suggestions regarding how to engage with Lao people as a visitor:

- Greet everyone with a grin and a "sabaidee" (hello).
- Respect the Lao culture and customs.
- Before photographing someone, obtain their permission.

- Compliments should be given freely.
- Learn to say "thank you" (khob khun) and "you're welcome" (mai pen rai) in Lao.

By following these guidelines, you may demonstrate to Lao people that you value their culture and want to learn more about it. They will appreciate your efforts, and you will have a more fun and gratifying stay as a result.

Here are some more things to consider while engaging with Lao people:

- Lao people are frequently hesitant towards strangers, thus establishing rapport may take some time.
- Lao people are highly respectful of the elderly, so be careful to show them respect.
- Because Lao people are typically humble, avoid being overly upfront or forceful.
- Lao people are highly family-oriented, so take an interest in theirs.

By following these guidelines, you may demonstrate to Lao people that you respect their culture and are interested in getting to know them. They will appreciate your efforts, and you will have a more fun and gratifying stay as a result.

Here are some activities you may participate in to learn more about Lao culture:

- Visit a nearby temple or watch.
- Attend a culinary lesson.
- Participate in a Lao festival.
- Learn a few Lao words.
- Learn about the history and culture of Laos.

By learning about Lao culture, you will be able to better understand and respect the Lao people. They are a fascinating and one-of-a-kind group of individuals who have a lot to offer tourists.

The Language of Laos

Lao is the official language of Laos, and it is spoken by around 60% of the people. It is also spoken in Isan, a region of northeastern Thailand. Because Lao is a tonal language, the meaning of a word might change depending on the tone with which it is uttered. Lao has five tones: high, low, rising, falling, and level.

The Lao Alphabet

The Lao alphabet is based on the Thai alphabet, however, it has a few more characters. There are 33 consonants and 5 vowels in the Lao alphabet. Thai consonants are pronounced similarly to English consonants. Vowels are pronounced similarly to Thai vowels, however, there are notable differences. When the vowel *"o"* is followed by a consonant, it is pronounced *"oo."*

Lao Expressions

Here are some simple Lao phrases you may find handy during your trip to Laos:

- Hello: Sabaidee (sah-bai-dee)
- Goodbye: La khwan (lah khwan)
- Thank you: Khop khun (khop khwan)
- You're welcome: Mai pen rai (mai pen rai)
- Excuse me: Khop khun khao (khop khwan kao)
- Please: Khop khun khao (khop khwan kao)
- How much is this?: Nee tao rai? (nee tao rai?)
- Do you speak English?: Khon thoi angkrit? (khon thoi angkrit?)
- I don't speak Lao: Khon mai bo pen Lao (khon mai bo pen Lao)

Where Can I Learn Lao?

Before visiting Laos, there are a few venues where you may study Lao. You can enroll in a class at a community college or an adult education program in your area. There are also a lot of online resources available to teach you the fundamentals of Lao.

When you arrive in Laos,

Once in Laos, you can continue to learn the language by conversing with the people. Most Lao people are quite nice and will gladly assist you in learning their language. Reading signs and menus might also help you learn certain Lao languages.

Lao Learning Tips

Here are some pointers for studying Lao:

- Begin with the fundamentals. Learn the alphabet, tones, and some fundamental phrases.
- Practice on a regular basis. The more you practice, the better your Lao will get.
- Make no apologies about making blunders. When learning a new language, everyone makes mistakes.
- Please be patient. Learning a new language takes time. Don't get disheartened if you don't learn Lao overnight.

Lao is a lovely and expressive language. Even learning a few basic Lao words will help you connect with the people and have a more real Laos experience.

The Religion of Laos

Laos is a Southeast Asian country with a rich and varied religious landscape. The major religion is Theravada Buddhism, which is followed by ethnic minority religions such as animism, Hinduism, and Christianity.

Theravada Buddhism

Laos' official religion is Theravada Buddhism, which is practiced by more than 80% of the people. It is a Buddhist lineage that focuses on personal liberation through the cultivation of knowledge and morality. Theravada Buddhists follow the teachings of the Four Noble Truths and the Eightfold Road, which offer a road to enlightenment.

Animism

Animism is a religious belief that all objects, both living and nonliving, have a spirit or soul. Many ethnic minority groups in Laos, including the Hmong, Mien, and Khmu, practice it. Animists believe that spirits may have an impact on their lives and that it is essential to satisfy them via sacrifices and ceremonies.

Hinduism

Hinduism is a minority religion in Laos, however, some ethnic groups, such as the Cham, practice it. Hindus believe in Brahman, the highest entity who is the source of all creation. They also believe in a reincarnation cycle in which souls are reincarnated into various bodies based on their karma.

Christianity

In Laos, Christianity is a minority religion, although it is gaining in popularity. Laos is home to a diverse range of Christian faiths, including Roman Catholicism, Protestantism, and Evangelicalism.

Christians believe in a single God who created the universe and sent his only son, Jesus Christ, to suffer for humanity's sins.

Religious Liberty

Laos is a secular republic that guarantees religious freedom. However, the government does ban religious activities that it considers to constitute a danger to national security on occasion. For example, the government has outlawed certain religious sects and has pushed down on unauthorized religious meetings.

Advice for Visitors

It is essential to observe the local religious norms when visiting Laos. This involves dressing modestly, abstaining from public displays of affection, and refraining from disparaging any faith. It's also a good idea to learn a few fundamental Lao words and phrases, such as "hello," "thank you," and "excuse me."

Here are some extra suggestions for Laos visitors:

- Respect holy places by not photographing or filming them without permission.
- In public, dress modestly, especially while visiting temples or other sacred locations.
- Avoid shows of love in public, such as embracing or kissing.
- Be aware of your words and refrain from making disparaging remarks about any faith.
- Learn a few basic Lao words and phrases.

By following these guidelines, you may help to guarantee that your trip to Laos is enjoyable and respectful.

The History of Laos

Laos is a Southeast Asian country that is landlocked. Thailand borders it on the west, Myanmar on the north, China on the northeast, Vietnam on the east, and Cambodia on the south. Laos is a hilly nation divided by the Annamite Range in the north and the Mekong River in the center. The Mon-Khmer people were Laos' first inhabitants. Lao, today's largest ethnic group in Laos, arrived around the 11th century. Fa Ngum established the Lan Xang kingdom in the 13th century, which grew to be one of Southeast Asia's greatest and most powerful. Lan Xang reigned for more than 400 years until being partitioned into three smaller kingdoms in the 18th century.

Laos became a French protectorate in the nineteenth century. The French dominated Laos for more than 50 years, bringing major changes to the country, including the development of roads, trains, and schools. Laos declared independence from France in 1945. The nation, however, was quickly engaged in civil conflict between the communist Pathet Lao and the royalist administration. The civil war lasted over 20 years and concluded with Pathet Lao's triumph in 1975. Laos has been a communist country since 1975. The administration has enacted a variety of socialist economic measures, as well as restrictions on free speech and assembly.

Laos, on the other hand, has made some headway in recent years and is currently one of Southeast Asia's fastest-growing economies. Laos is a lovely and intriguing country with a long history. It is home to a variety of distinct cultures and customs, and it is a popular tourist attraction. If you're going to Laos, make sure to study about its history and culture. *The following are some of the most significant events in Lao history:*

- Fa Ngum established the Lan Xang kingdom in 1353.
- Lan Xang was partitioned by three minor kingdoms in 1707.
- Laos became a French protectorate in 1893.
- Laos declared independence from France in 1945.
- The Geneva Accords were signed in 1954, thereby ending the First Indochina War.
- The Pathet Lao launched a guerrilla campaign against the royalist regime in 1960.

- 1975: The Lao People's Democratic Republic was established after Pathet Lao won the civil war.
- The New Economic Mechanism was launched in 1986, signaling a transition away from a centrally planned economy.
- Laos joined the Association of Southeast Asian Nations (ASEAN) in 1997.
- 2004: The Lao government initiates a political reform process.
- Laos will host the Southeast Asian Games in 2013.
- Laos attained lower-middle-income status in 2016.
- Laos will commemorate its 50th anniversary of independence in 2023.

Laos has a lengthy and complicated history. It has been inspired by many different civilizations and has lived through both peace and conflict. Laos is now a lovely and tranquil country that is steadily opening up to the rest of the globe.

If you want to visit, read about its history and culture first. You will be rewarded with a memorable and one-of-a-kind experience.

Copyrighted Material

CHAPTER 1

Introduction to Laos

Laos, formally known as the Lao People's Democratic Republic, is a landlocked Southeast Asian country. Laos is a hidden jewel that provides a unique combination of natural beauty, rich cultural legacy, and friendly hospitality. It is bordered by China to the north, Vietnam to the east, Cambodia to the southeast, Thailand to the west, and Myanmar to the northwest. Laos, with a population of over 7 million people, is noted for its relaxed culture, breathtaking scenery, and historic temples.

Laos is distinguished geographically by its rugged topography, lush forests, and the massive Mekong River, which runs across the nation from north to south. The Mekong River is not only a lifeline for the people of Laos, but it is also a significant tourist destination, with river cruises, kayaking, and visiting the gorgeous riverbanks available.

Laos's rich cultural legacy is one of its most intriguing features. The nation has a lengthy history that dates back thousands of years, influenced by many civilizations such as the Khmer Empire and the French colonial era. Vientiane, the capital city, is a great combination of old-world beauty and modern growth. Visitors may tour old temples like Wat Si Saket and Pha That Luang, which are important religious and historical monuments, while they are here.

Another must-see location in Laos is Luang Prabang, which is a UNESCO World Heritage Site. This old mountain town is noted for its well-preserved Buddhist temples, medieval architecture, and lively night markets. The alms-giving ceremony, in which Buddhist monks collect donations from residents and visitors, is an unforgettable spiritual experience. Laos is a treasure for nature enthusiasts. Several national parks, notably Nam Ha National Protected Area and Phou Hin Poun National Biodiversity Conservation Area, are located in the country and provide possibilities for trekking, animal viewing, and exploring pristine ecosystems.

Another unusual destination that reflects Laos' fascinating past is the Plain of Jars, a strange archaeological site littered with ancient stone jars.

Laos is also noted for its numerous ethnic groups, each with its unique set of traditions and customs. The Lao people, who make up the bulk of the population, are noted for their pleasant attitude and great hospitality. Visitors may immerse themselves in the local culture by taking part in traditional festivities such as Boun Pi Mai (Lao New Year) and Boun Bang Fai (Rocket Festival), which are celebrated with music, dancing, and colorful processions by the people.

Laotian cuisine is a delectable blend of flavors influenced by neighboring Thailand, Vietnam, and China. Sticky rice, known as khao niao in Laos, is a staple snack that is frequently served with a variety of foods, including spicy papaya salad (tam mak hoong) and laap, a minced beef salad seasoned with herbs and spices. Foodies may also enjoy delectable street cuisine and visit the colorful night markets, where they can taste local specialties and connect with friendly merchants.

Laos has grown in popularity as a tourist destination in recent years, drawing visitors looking for a genuine and off-the-beaten-path experience. The country's natural beauty, cultural richness, and friendly friendliness make it a perfect destination for anyone wishing to venture beyond the well-trodden tourist paths in Southeast Asia.

Finally, Laos is a wonderful country that combines natural beauty, a rich cultural legacy, and kind friendliness. Laos offers something for everyone, from historic temples and gorgeous scenery to busy markets and delectable cuisine. Whether you're looking for adventure, leisure, or cultural immersion, Laos is a location that won't disappoint. So pack your luggage and prepare for an incredible adventure through Southeast Asia's heart.

What is There to See and Do in Laos?

Laos is a Southeast Asian landlocked country surrounded by Thailand to the west, Cambodia to the south, Vietnam to the east, and China to the north. It is a tiny nation, having a population of just more than 7 million people. Laos is a lovely nation with a fascinating culture and history. It has beautiful landscapes, such as mountains, rivers, waterfalls, and woods. There are also several historic temples and ruins to discover. Laos is an excellent destination for outdoor enthusiasts. Hiking, biking, kayaking, rafting, and fishing are all options. You can also go to national parks and animal refuges. Laos has a lot to offer in terms of cultural experiences. Throughout the year, there are several traditional festivals and events. You may also tour communities and learn directly about Laotian culture.

Here are some of the top sights and activities in Laos:

Visit Luang Prabang: Luang Prabang, a UNESCO World Heritage Site and one of Laos' most famous tourist attractions. Many temples, monasteries, and palaces may be found throughout the city. Hiking, motorcycling, and exploring the surrounding countryside are among popular activities.

Trek across the Annamite Mountains: The Annamite Mountains are a mountain range in Laos and Vietnam. There are several walking paths in the highlands that provide breathtaking views of the surrounding area.

Visit the Pak Ou Caverns: The Pak Ou Caves are a collection of caverns on the Mekong River. Thousands of Buddha sculptures may be seen in the caverns.

Float along the Mekong River: The Mekong River is one of Southeast Asia's major rivers. You may enjoy the landscape by taking a boat ride along the river.

Visit the Plain of Jars: The Plain of Jars is a Laos archaeological site. Thousands of stone jars of uncertain provenance can be found at the site.

Discover Laotian culture: There are several possibilities to discover Laotian culture. Villages may be visited, festivals can be attended, and traditional arts and crafts can be learned.

Laotian cuisine: This is a delectable combination of Thai, Vietnamese, and Chinese cuisine. Try the local favorites including laap (a spicy minced pork salad), khao soi (a curry noodle soup), and sticky rice.

Discover the Laotian way of life: Laos is a slow-paced country with a laid-back attitude. Take some time to unwind and appreciate the little things in life.

Laos is an excellent destination for anyone who likes the environment, culture, and history. It is a lovely nation with much to offer visitors.

Here are some more suggestions for arranging your vacation to Laos:

- The dry season, which lasts from November to April, is the greatest time to visit Laos.
- Although Lao is the official language of Laos, English is extensively used in tourist regions.
- Laos' currency is the kip.
- Tipping is not customary in Laos.
- Make sure to sample some of the local cuisine. Laotian cuisine is wonderful!
- Laos is a safe place to visit. However, it is critical to be aware of the dangers of unexploded ordnance (UXO) in certain places.

When is the Best Time to Visit Laos?

As a tourist considering a trip to Laos in 2024, you must determine the optimal time to come to maximize your experience. This guide will walk you through the seasons and highlight the best time to visit this lovely nation.

Dry Season (November to April)

Laos's dry season is the most popular time to visit. The weather is pleasant and sunny, with temperatures ranging from 75 to 85 degrees Fahrenheit on average. This time of year has relatively little rain, making it great for outdoor activities like hiking, riding, and river cruises. The dry season is also the greatest time to visit Laos' many temples and historical monuments.

Shoulder Season (October and May)

Laos' shoulder seasons are a suitable compromise between the dry and rainy seasons. With typical temperatures ranging from 70 to 80 degrees Fahrenheit, the weather remains nice.

There is also less rain than during the rainy season. However, during the shoulder seasons, costs and crowds are reduced, making them a suitable alternative for budget travelers or those who prefer less congested areas.

Rainy Season (May to October)
Laos' rainy season is distinguished by hot, humid weather and regular rains. During this period, the average temperature is 80 degrees Fahrenheit. While rain might make certain outdoor activities challenging, it also has its own allure. During this season, the lush foliage is at its peak, and the waterfalls are in full flow. The rainy season is also an excellent time to view the country's wildlife because many animals become more active during the rainy season.

Whatever time of year you visit Laos, you will have an unforgettable experience. Natural beauty, cultural legacy, and kind people abound throughout the nation.

Here are some more things to think about while arranging your vacation to Laos:

Festivals: Throughout the year, Laos organizes a number of festivals, many of which are tied to Buddhism. The Luang Festival, held in November in Vientiane, is the most well-known.

Peak travel season: The dry season (November to April) is the most popular time to visit Laos. If you want to travel during this period, make sure to reserve your lodgings and activities ahead of time.

Travel during the off-season: The rainy season (May to October) is Laos' off-season. While costs and crowds are reduced during this period, keep in mind that some outdoor activities may be limited due to weather.

Finally, the perfect time to visit Laos is when your interests and finances coincide. With so much to see and do in this lovely nation, you will have a fantastic time no matter when you visit.

Here are some more suggestions for arranging your vacation to Laos:

- Learn some fundamental Lao phrases. This will demonstrate your appreciation for the local culture and make communication with locals simpler.
- Be prepared for high temperatures and humidity. Because Laos is a tropical country, the weather may be hot and humid all year. Pack light clothing and sunscreen, and stay hydrated.
- Be mindful of Buddhist culture. Laos is a Buddhist nation, therefore dress modestly and avoid making loud sounds or engaging in inappropriate behavior.
- Local companies should be supported. Try to eat at local restaurants, shop at local markets, and support local tour operators while in Laos. This will assist in improving the local economy and guarantee that your money is directed to those in most need.

What to pack for your trip to Laos

It is critical to consider the time of year you will be visiting Laos while preparing for your vacation. Laos has two distinct seasons: dry (November to April) and rainy (May to October). You may take lighter clothing if you travel during the dry season. Most activities will require only shorts, t-shirts, and sandals. If you intend to go hiking or trekking, you will need to bring more appropriate attire. Hiking boots, long trousers, and a light jacket are all required.

If you visit during the rainy season, you will need to bring additional rain gear. A raincoat, umbrella, and water-resistant shoes are required. You should also bring a change of clothes in case you are trapped in a deluge. In addition to clothing, you will need to pack a few more items for your trip to Laos. *These are some examples:*

Clothing

- A blend of lightweight, loose-fitting shirts with short and long sleeves.
- Shorts that dry quickly during travel.
- A jacket that is lightweight and waterproof.
- Sneakers and sandals that breathe.
- Hiking socks made of merino wool and quick-dry undergarments.
- Optional sarong or sarong skirt.
- Sunglasses and a hat.

Because Laos has a tropical environment, bring light clothes that are suitable for hot and humid weather. Pack a variety of short- and long-sleeved shirts, as it may get cool in the night, especially in the highlands. You should also bring a lightweight waterproof jacket on wet days.

For strolling throughout cities and towns, breathable shoes are great. You should also bring sandals for wearing in hot weather or at the beach. If you intend to go hiking or trekking, bring a decent pair of hiking boots with you.

Accessories

- A water bottle that is large but lightweight.
- Repellent for insects.
- Sunscreen.
- Toiletries.
- Chargers and camera.
- First-aid supplies.
- Passports, visas, and other travel documentation are required.
- Keep your valuables safe with a money belt or bag.

It's critical to remain hydrated in Laos, so bring a big water bottle. You should also bring insect repellent and sunscreen to protect yourself from the sun and insects. Toiletries, a camera, and chargers, a first-aid kit, and your passport, visa, and other travel documents are also required.

Other things to think about

- If you intend to cook, you should bring a small portable burner and cooking tools.
- If you intend to visit isolated locations, you should have a torch or headlamp.
- If you intend to go hiking or trekking, you need to have a daypack and other hiking equipment.
- Pack any drugs you take on a regular basis.

What should you leave at home?

- Because you'll be doing a lot of walking, leave bulky clothing items at home.
- Keep expensive jewelry and other valuables at home, as they may be stolen.
- Leave superfluous devices at home; they will just add to the weight of your suitcase.
- Although Laos is a generally secure nation, it's always a good idea to stay aware of your surroundings and take care to avoid theft and other crimes. You can guarantee that you have everything you need for a safe and pleasurable vacation to Laos by packing intelligently.

Here are some extra packing suggestions for your Laos trip:

- Pack light clothes made of natural fibers like cotton and linen. In hot weather, these textiles will keep you cool and comfortable.
- Bring a few pairs of suitable walking shoes.
- Pack a hat and sunglasses to shield yourself from the sun.
- Pack insect repellent to keep mosquitoes and other pests at bay.
- Keep a modest first-aid kit on hand in case of minor injuries.
- Pack a duplicate of your passport and other vital travel papers in case they are misplaced or stolen.

Laos travel essentials

As a traveler wanting to visit Laos in 2024, you must be well-prepared to make the most of your vacation. In this guide, we will go over the travel necessities you should think about before going on your journey to this wonderful place.

Entry Requirements & Visas:

Before you travel to Laos, it is critical that you understand the country's visa requirements. Many nations might receive a visa on arrival as of September 2021, according to my knowledge. However, laws and restrictions might change, so it's best to check the official website of the Lao Embassy or consulate in your country for the most up-to-date information and to get the necessary visa well in advance.

Travel Insurance:

Travel insurance is a non-negotiable need for every foreign travel, and Laos is no exception. Medical crises and unforeseeable disasters may occur anywhere. Having comprehensive travel insurance will offer you financial protection and peace of mind throughout your travels.

Health Precautions:

Before visiting Laos, see your healthcare professional to verify you are up to date on any essential immunizations. Malaria, dengue fever, and other tropical illnesses are common in the area, so bring insect repellant and proper clothes. To avoid waterborne infections, stay hydrated and drink bottled or boiled water.

Packing Tips:

The climate in Laos ranges from tropical in the plains to chilly in the highlands. Pack light, breathable clothing for hot, humid days, as well as a light jacket for colder evenings. Remember to bring strong walking shoes for seeing temples and natural areas, as well as a swimsuit if you intend to swim in Laos' spectacular waterfalls and swimming holes.

Respect for Cultural Diversity:

Laos has a rich cultural legacy that is strongly entwined with Theravada Buddhism. It is necessary to dress modestly when visiting temples and religious locations, covering shoulders and knees. Remove your shoes before entering the temple grounds, and always seek permission before photographing monks or religious rituals.

Local Etiquette:

Laos is recognized for its kind people. Locals should be greeted with a *"sabaidee"* (hello) and a courteous nod. Handshakes are popular, but remember that the head is regarded as the most holy portion of the body, while the feet are considered the least sacred. Keep your feet from pointing at people or religious items.

Currency & Payment:

The official currency is the Lao Kip (LAK), however Thai Baht and US Dollars are frequently accepted in tourist regions. However, it is best to keep small denominations of Kip on hand for local markets and small companies. Credit cards are accepted in big institutions, while cash is recommended in rural regions.

Communication:

Communication is quite simple in Laos, particularly in metropolitan areas. Local SIM cards, which offer reasonable data plans to keep you connected during your vacation, may be obtained at the airport or via mobile network providers. Additionally, because English may not be frequently spoken in distant locations, consider installing translation applications to assist in conversation.

Transportation:

Laos' transportation network has grown over time, providing a variety of choices for moving about. Tuk-tuks are a common mode of transportation for short trips inside communities, whereas buses and minivans link big cities. If you're feeling daring, hire a motorcycle, but be sure you have the proper license and practice caution on the roadways.

Local Cuisine:

Lao cuisine is a delectable combination of fresh ingredients and fragrant herbs.

Sticky rice is a popular side dish, frequently paired with delicious dips and curries. Try the *"laap,"* a classic minced beef salad, and the "tam mak hoong," a spicy green papaya salad. Accept the native habit of sharing meals and savor the burst of flavors that characterize Lao cuisine.

Exploring Nature:

Laos is well-known for its beautiful scenery and natural beauty. Luang Prabang, a UNESCO World Heritage site, is known for its beautiful waterfalls, lush forests, and the majestic Mekong River. Vang Vieng is known for its stunning limestone structures and adventure sports like kayaking and rock climbing. Take a leisurely boat down the Mekong River to see rural life unfold along its banks for a genuinely unique experience.

Souvenirs & marketplaces:

The marketplaces of Laos are a treasure trove of handicrafts, fabrics, and one-of-a-kind souvenirs. The Talat Sao Morning Market in Vientiane is great for silk textile buying, while the Night Market in Luang Prabang is well-known for its handwoven goods and indigenous artwork. Remember to negotiate politely and to patronize local craftspeople.

Finally, Laos in 2024 promises an enthralling voyage through a nation rich in cultural diversity and natural beauty. You may guarantee that your vacation is not only memorable but also culturally sensitive by embracing local customs, honoring traditions, and rigorous planning. Prepare to be enchanted by Laos' tranquil beauty, colorful marketplaces, and genuine kindness of its people - a travel experience that will last long after you've left its borders.

Where to Stay in Laos

Finding the ideal lodging for a trip to Laos in 2024 is critical for a pleasant experience. This guide will provide you with an overview of the top locations to stay in Laos, as well as their prices, so you can make an educated selection.

Luang Prabang: A UNESCO World Heritage site, Luang Prabang is a renowned tourist destination in Laos. It provides a variety of lodging alternatives to accommodate a variety of budgets. There are upmarket resorts and boutique hotels with costs ranging from $150 to $500 per night for luxury seekers. Mid-range hotels and guesthouses may be purchased for $50 to $150 per night, while hostels and guesthouses can be found for as little as $10 to $30 per night.

Vientiane: As Laos' capital city, Vientiane combines contemporary conveniences with traditional treasures. Accommodation choices in this area appeal to a wide range of budgets. In Vientiane, luxury hotels and resorts may cost between $100 and $300 per night. Mid-range hotels and guesthouses cost between $40 and $100 a night, while hostels and guesthouses cost between $10 and $30 per night.

Luang Namtha: For nature lovers and thrill seekers, Luang Namtha is a must-see site in Laos. This area is well-known for its hiking and ecotourism options.

Accommodation in Luang Namtha is reasonably priced, with guesthouses and cheap hotels ranging in price from $10 to $50 per night. Mid-range selections vary from $50 to $100 each night.

Vang Vieng: Nestled among gorgeous limestone mountains and the Nam Song River, Vang Vieng is a popular destination for outdoor sports and travelers. Accommodation in Vang Vieng is available for a variety of budgets. Budget guesthouses and hostels cost between $10 and $30 per night. Mid-priced hotels and resorts vary from $30 to $100 per night.

Pakse: This is a gateway to the Bolaven Plateau and the famed 4,000 Islands area in southern Laos. Pakse has a wide range of accommodation alternatives, with costs to match. Luxury hotels and resorts may range in price from $100 to $300 per night. Mid-range hotels and guesthouses cost between $30 and $100 a night, while budget choices cost between $10 and $30 per night.

Don Det: Don Det, one of the Mekong River's 4,000 islands, is a calm haven for visitors seeking leisure and natural beauty. Don Det's accommodation is primarily made up of guesthouses and bungalows. Prices here are reasonably priced, ranging from $10 to $50 each night.

Muang Ngoi: Muang Ngoi, a little town tucked beside the Nam Ou River, provides a calm respite from the hustle and bustle of the metropolis. Muang Ngoi's lodging options are few yet lovely. Bungalows and guesthouses may be obtained for $10 to $50 per night.

Laos has a variety of lodging alternatives to meet any visitor's budget and interests. Laos has something for everyone, whether you're seeking luxury resorts, mid-range hotels, cheap guesthouses, or backpacker hostels. With the pricing ranges listed above in mind, you can plan your trip to Laos in 2024 and make the most of your time there.

Budgeting for Your Laos Trip

Laos provides a one-of-a-kind vacation experience. However, in order to get the most out of your trip, you must carefully arrange your spending. This guide will go through several areas of budgeting for your Laos vacation, such as lodging, transportation, food, activities, and incidental costs.

Accommodation: There are alternatives for every budget when it comes to lodging in Laos. There are a variety of options available, ranging from luxury resorts to inexpensive guesthouses and hostels. A mid-range hotel room in Laos costs roughly $30-50 per night, while budget choices can cost as little as $10-20 per night. Consider reserving ahead of time to get the greatest bargains, and check costs on different travel websites.

Transportation: Getting around Laos may be an adventure in and of itself. Buses, tuk-tuks, and taxis are the most prevalent types of transportation for guests.

Buses are the most cost-effective choice, with short-distance costs ranging from $1 to $5. Tuk-tuks are a common mode of transportation for short excursions inside cities and can cost between $2 and $5 for each ride. Taxis are more costly, with costs beginning at $5 and increasing in accordance with distance. To avoid unpleasant surprises, it is best to negotiate the fee before boarding a tuk-tuk or cab.

Cuisine: Laos is well-known for its tasty and reasonably priced street cuisine. Noodle soups, grilled meats, and fresh fruits are among the many foods available in local markets and street booths. A meal from a street seller will often cost between $1 and $3. If you want to eat out, expect to pay between $5 and $10 for each meal. Consider dining where the locals dine and sampling traditional Lao food to save money.

Activities: Laos has a wide range of activities for visitors, from viewing ancient temples to trekking through beautiful jungles. Many attractions charge an admission fee, which can range from $1 to $10 per person. Popular activities such as boat rides along the Mekong River and visits to the Kuang Si Waterfalls may be significantly more expensive. It is best to explore and prioritize the things that you are most interested in before allocating your funds.

Miscellaneous Expenses: In addition to the basic expenses, it is important to account for any additional charges that may develop during your trip. Visa fees, travel insurance, souvenirs, and gratuities are examples of them. Most nations may get a visa on arrival in Laos, with costs ranging from $30 to $50 depending on the length of your stay. Travel insurance is strongly advised to protect against any unforeseen occurrences and can cost between $5 and $10 per day. Remember to budget for souvenirs and tips, as it is traditional in Laos to tip service personnel.

Budgeting Suggestions:

- Research and plan your schedule ahead of time to have a good sense of the costs involved.

- Consider traveling during the off-season to benefit from reduced pricing.
- To save money, choose public transportation such as buses and tuk-tuks instead of private cabs.
- Eat at local markets and street vendors for traditional Lao food at low costs.
- Look for lodging discounts and book ahead of time to get the best pricing.
- Carry a reusable water bottle to save money on bottled water, as tap water in Laos is unsafe to drink.

Planning a budget for your Laos vacation is essential for ensuring a wonderful and financially doable experience. You may efficiently manage your budget by taking into account lodging, transportation, food, activities, and miscellaneous costs. Remember to be adaptable and budget for additional expenditures, since unexpected possibilities may emerge during your travel. You may make the most of your stay in Laos and create lasting memories with careful planning and a well-managed budget.

Here are some budgetary recommendations for your Laos trip:

- Stay in hostels or guesthouses: The cheapest option to stay in Laos is at a hostel or a guesthouse. Dorm beds are frequently available for roughly $5 per night, and individual rooms for around $15 per night.
- Consume street food: Eating street food is an excellent method to save money on meals in Laos. Delicious lunches may be found for roughly $1.
- Take local transit: The cheapest method to go to Laos is to take local transportation. There are buses, minivans, and tuk-tuks available.
- Do free and low-cost activities: Hiking, biking, swimming, and visiting temples are just a few of the free and low-cost activities available in Laos.
- Plan your activities ahead of time: Planning your activities ahead of time will help you save money. When you arrange activities ahead of time, you may often get savings.

- Shop around for souvenirs: Although souvenirs are inexpensive in Laos, you may save money by shopping around.
- Tipping is not expected in Laos, so avoid it. If you wish to tip, a little sum is appropriate.

By following these suggestions, you may easily budget for an economical and delightful trip to Laos.

Getting Ready for Your Laos Trip

A journey to Laos in 2024 promises to be an entertaining and educational experience. Laos, located in Southeast Asia, provides a unique combination of natural beauty, a rich cultural legacy, and kind friendliness. To make the most of your stay, you must plan ahead of time. This book will give you crucial recommendations and insights to ensure that your vacation to Laos is enjoyable and trouble-free.

Itinerary planning and research: Conduct an extensive study of the country's history, culture, and attractions before going on your Laos vacation. Make a precise itinerary that includes must-see places like Luang Prabang, Vientiane, and the Plain of Jars. Consider the length of your vacation, the weather, and any special events or festivals that will be taking place during your stay.

Visa and Travel Documents: Make sure your passport is valid for at least six months beyond the date of your scheduled travel. Check your nationality's visa requirements and apply for a visa well in advance. Many nations are eligible for visa-on-arrival in Laos; nonetheless, it is always essential to clarify the most recent requirements with the nearest Lao embassy or consulate.

Health & vaccines: For the most up-to-date information on recommended vaccines for Laos, see your healthcare practitioner or a travel clinic. Hepatitis A and B, typhoid, tetanus, and diphtheria are all common immunizations. If you want to visit rural or isolated places, consider taking anti-malarial medicine.

Travel Insurance: Purchase comprehensive travel insurance that covers medical emergencies, trip cancellations, and lost items. If you want to indulge in adventurous activities such as trekking or river rafting during your vacation, be sure your insurance policy covers such activities.

Packing Essentials: Pack lightweight, breathable clothing appropriate for Laos' tropical environment. Remember to bring sunscreen, bug repellant, a hat, and appropriate walking shoes. When visiting temples, wear modest clothes that cover your shoulders and knees. A robust backpack and a universal power adaptor are also suggested.

Language and Cultural Etiquette: While English is widely spoken in key tourist sites, learning a few simple words in Lao can considerably enhance your experience and interactions with locals. Respect local norms and traditions, such as taking off your shoes before entering temples or residences, and dressing modestly while visiting religious places.

Currency and Financial Concerns: The Lao kip (LAK) is the country's official currency. While credit cards are accepted in bigger places, carrying cash is recommended, especially in rural regions. abms are commonly accessible in large cities, but having some local cash on hand is usually a smart idea. Inform your bank of your trip intentions to avoid problems with your credit cards.

Transportation: Laos has an extensive domestic aviation, bus, and boat network. Consider reserving domestic flights ahead of time to get the cheapest prices. Within cities, tuk-tuks and taxis are common forms of transportation, while motorbikes and bicycles may be leased to explore smaller towns and rural regions.

Safety and Security: Laos is typically a secure nation for travelers, although it's always a good idea to take precautions. Keep your things protected, be alert, and avoid lonely locations late at night. To avoid health problems, stay hydrated, drink bottled water, and practice basic cleanliness.

Respect for Nature and Local Communities: Laos is endowed with breathtaking natural features such as waterfalls, caverns, and national parks. Respect the environment by not polluting and adhering to established routes. Participate in ethical tourist activities and support local businesses to help the local economy.

Planning ahead of time for your Laos vacation in 2024 will ensure a smooth and pleasurable visit to this fascinating nation. You will be well-equipped to immerse yourself in the beauty and charm of Laos if you undertake sufficient study, secure essential travel papers, and observe local customs. Accept the warmth of the Lao people, savor the delectable cuisine, and make memories that last a lifetime.

Here are some more preparation advice for your Laos trip in 2024:

- Hire a local guide to assist you in planning your vacation and navigating the nation.

- Be mindful of the dangers of malaria and other tropical illnesses, and take precautions.
- Be prepared for power outages and other inconveniences.
- Tipping is not expected, but it is valued in Laos.
- In marketplaces, bargaining is widespread, so don't be scared to haggle.
- Make sure to taste the local cuisine! Lao food is both excellent and diverse.

Memories From My Laos Trip

Date: Destination:

NOTE

CHAPTER 2

How to Choose Your Laos Itinerary

As a visitor considering a trip to Laos in 2024, it's essential to arrange an itinerary that allows you to maximize your time and explore the many attractions that this lovely nation has to offer. This book aims to give you helpful insights and recommendations on how to plan an enjoyable journey in Laos.

Research and Understand Laos: Take the time to investigate and comprehend the country's geography, climate, culture, and history before selecting your schedule. Laos is famed for its breathtaking scenery, which includes the Mekong River, lush forests, and scenic mountains. Learn about the various areas, such as Luang Prabang, Vientiane, and the Bolaven Plateau, to get a sense of what they have to offer.

Determine the length of your journey: Determine how long you intend to remain in Laos. The nation has a lot to offer, so make sure you plan enough time to visit all of its attractions. It is advised that you spend at least one week covering the highlights, but if you have more time, you may explore deeper into the country's hidden gems.

Prioritize Your Interests: Laos has something for everyone, including history, culture, adventure, and environment. Determine your choices and prioritize the activities and attractions that appeal to you. The UNESCO World Heritage monuments at Luang Prabang and the Plain of Jars in Xieng Khouang are must-see destinations for history buffs. Adventurers can visit the breathtaking Kuang Si Waterfalls or go on a multi-day trek in the northern highlands.

Explore the Cultural Heritage: Laos has a rich cultural past, and it is essential to immerse oneself in its traditions and practices. To experience the spiritual side of Laos, attend the daily alms-giving ceremony in Luang Prabang, visit the historic temples of Vientiane, or participate in a traditional Baci ceremony.

Balance Your Itinerary: While it may be tempting to pack as many sites as possible into your schedule, it is critical to create a balance between discovery and leisure. Allow yourself time to unwind and absorb in the calm surroundings because Laos is famed for its laid-back vibe. Consider spending a few days in Luang Prabang, where you may explore the night markets, take a boat ride down the Mekong River, or simply relax at a riverbank café.

Consider the Season: Because Laos has multiple seasons, it's critical to organize your trip around the weather. The dry season, which runs from November to April, is widely seen to be the finest time to visit, with comfortable temperatures and clear skies. However, if you want to see the brilliant vegetation and rich sceneries, the rainy season (May to October) may provide an unforgettable experience.

Seek Local suggestions: To improve your Laos itinerary, ask locals or experienced travelers who have visited the nation for suggestions. They may offer unique insights, advocate off-the-beaten-path places, and advise real cultural experiences not available in guidebooks.

Schedule Your Transportation: Because Laos has a relatively poor transportation system, it is critical to schedule your transportation ahead of time. Depending on the distances you need to cover, consider whether you want to travel by bus, boat, or domestic aircraft. Hiring a local guide or driver can also be advantageous since they can negotiate the country's roads and give useful information along the journey.

Be adaptable: While having a well-planned schedule is vital, remaining flexible is key. Unexpected possibilities may present themselves, and you may uncover hidden treasures that were not on your initial itinerary. Embrace spontaneity and give yourself permission to depart from the agenda if something piques your attention.

<u>If you are considering a vacation to Laos in 2024, here are some suggestions for your itinerary:</u>

- Determine your passions. What are you most excited to see and do in Laos? Do you want to learn more about the country's history and culture? Hike through the mountains? Do you want to unwind on the beach? You may begin to restrict your possibilities after you know what you are interested in.

- Take into account the season. The climate of Laos is tropical, with hot, humid summers and colder winters. The dry season, from November to April, is the greatest time to visit. However, if you want to view the Mekong River in full flow, you should go during the wet season, which runs from May to October.
- Make a budget. Laos is a very inexpensive nation to visit, but it is still vital to plan ahead of time. This will assist you in deciding where to stay, what to eat, and what activities to participate in.
- Reserve your flights and lodging. Once you've created a general plan, it's time to start arranging flights and lodging. Laos is served by a number of airlines, and there are several hotels, guesthouses, and homestays to select from.
- Do your homework. There is a plethora of information on Laos available online. Read

blogs, travel guides, and forums for itinerary inspiration and information on the finest areas to visit.
- Be adaptable. When traveling, things don't always go as planned, so being adaptable is essential. Be prepared to adjust your plans if a flight is canceled or a natural calamity strikes.
- Relax and have a good time! Laos is a lovely nation with plenty to offer visitors. Take in the ambiance, meet the locals, and create experiences that last a lifetime.

Here are some itineraries for a vacation to Laos in 2024:

This 7-day trip contains a combination of cultural and natural attractions:

1. Spend two days in Luang Prabang, touring the UNESCO World Heritage Site and taking in the relaxed environment.
2.

3. Visit the Pak Ou Caves for a day excursion to see hundreds of Buddha pictures.
4. Hike to Mount Phou Si for panoramic views of the city.
5. Visit the Kuang Si Waterfalls, which are popular for swimming and picnics.
6. Spend the day visiting Vang Vieng, a town noted for its caverns, rivers, and limestone cliffs.
7. Take a Mekong River boat tour to explore communities, animals, and floating marketplaces.

<u>10-day itinerary: This plan includes a lengthier stay in Luang Prabang as well as visits to some of Laos's more distant areas:</u>

As previously said, spend three days in Luang Prabang.

1. Take a three-day trip across the Annapurna Mountains to explore breathtaking landscapes and quaint towns.

2. Visit the Plain of Jars, an enigmatic archaeological site containing thousands of stone jars.
3.
4. Spend a few days in Thakhek, a town famous for its caverns and waterfalls.
5. Take a Mekong River boat journey to the town of Pakse.
6. Visit the Bolaven Plateau, which is noted for its waterfalls and coffee plantations.
7. Spend a few days in Vientiane, the capital, before flying home.

Of course, these are just a few ideas. There are plenty of additional things to do in Laos. The most essential thing is to select an itinerary that is both interesting to you and falls within your price and time limits. No matter how you spend your time in Laos, you will have a wonderful experience. The nation is full of nice people, stunning landscapes, and an intriguing culture. So, what are you holding out for? Begin arranging your trip right away!

Visas and Currency Exchange

If you want to visit Laos in 2024, you should be informed of the visa requirements and currency conversion processes to guarantee a pleasant and trouble-free journey. We will give you all of the relevant information on visas and currency exchange in Laos for the year 2024 in this guide.

Visas for Laos:

Visitors to Laos will need a visa starting in 2024 unless they come from one of the visa-exempt nations. Laos' visa policy is subject to change, so check with the nearest Lao embassy or consulate for the most up-to-date information before your travel.

Visa-Free Countries: For a limited time, citizens of certain nations can enter Laos without a visa. ASEAN member nations, Russia, Switzerland, Japan, South Korea, and some European countries are among these countries as of 2024. Depending on nationality, the visa-free duration ranges from 14 to 90 days. It is important to remember, however, that the visa exemption is subject to change, therefore it is critical to confirm the current requirements before your travel.

Visa on Arrival: For travelers from non-visa-exempt countries, Laos provides visa-on-arrival services at international airports and certain land border crossings. You can stay in Laos for up to 30 days with a visa on arrival. A valid passport with at least six months' validity, a recent passport-sized photograph, and a visa cost in US dollars (cash only) are required to receive a visa on arrival.

E-Visa: Visitors to Laos can also obtain an e-visa. The e-visa allows you to apply for a visa online before your travel, removing the requirement for a visa on arrival. Citizens of qualified countries can get an e-visa for a maximum stay of 30 days. The application procedure is simple, and you will be emailed your e-visa, which you may print and produce upon arrival in Laos.

Laos Currency Exchange: Laos' national currency is the Lao Kip (LAK). Despite the fact that the Lao Kip is the official currency, US dollars are routinely accepted in major tourist locations, hotels, and bigger institutions.

However, bring some Lao Kip with you for minor purchases and while visiting local markets or rural regions where US dollars may not be accepted.

<u>Here are some important things to remember about currency conversion in Laos:</u>

Currency Exchange: Currency exchange services are widely available in Laos, especially in large cities and tourism destinations. Currency exchange services are provided by banks, authorized money changers, and hotels. For better prices and security, it is suggested that you convert your currency to approved money changers or banks.

US Dollars: The most generally recognized foreign currency in Laos is the US dollar. For convenience, bring US currency in small amounts (ideally $1, $5, $10, and $20 notes). Check that the bills are in excellent condition; ripped or damaged banknotes may not be accepted.

Withdrawals from abms: ATMs are commonly available in major towns and tourism regions across Laos. The majority of abms only accept Lao Kip, although some also accept US dollars. However, keep in mind that abms may have withdrawal limitations and levy transaction fees, so check with your bank about overseas withdrawal fees before your trip.

Credit Cards: In Laos, upmarket hotels, restaurants, and bigger institutions accept credit cards. However, carrying cash is usually a smart idea because smaller places and local markets may not take credit cards. In addition, notify your bank of your vacation intentions to avoid any problems with card usage.

Currency Exchange Rates: Because currency exchange rates in Laos frequently fluctuate, it's best to compare prices at several exchange counters before completing a purchase. Furthermore, be wary of unregistered money changers who may provide tempting rates but may be engaged in fraudulent operations.

Currency Exchange Tips

- Currency should always be exchanged in a bank or money exchange agency.
- Avoid exchanging currencies at hotels or businesses since the exchange rate will be lower.
- Before exchanging currencies, check the current exchange rate.
- Carry modest denominations of cash since changing big bills might be challenging.
- Keep your exchange receipts in case you need to convert your kip to your native currency after you depart Laos.

Using ATMs and Credit Cards

- Although credit cards and abms are generally accepted in Laos, it is always a good idea to keep some cash on hand because not all shops take credit cards.
- Visa and Mastercard are the most commonly accepted credit cards in Laos. American Express and Diners Club are less popular.

- Most major cities and towns in Laos have abms. abms often take Visa and Mastercard, however, it is always better to double-check before using one.

Tips for Using ATMs and Credit Cards

- Keep your credit card and PIN number secure at all times.
- Credit cards should not be used at abms situated in remote places.
- Keep an eye out for ABM skimming frauds.
- Report any lost or stolen credit cards to your credit card company right away.

Travel Insurance

When visiting Laos, it is critical to have travel insurance. Medical bills, trip cancellations, and other unanticipated circumstances are all covered by travel insurance.

When selecting travel insurance coverage, check the tiny print to ensure that it covers all of your needs.

Travel Insurance Buying Advice

- Compare insurance from various companies.
- Check if the policy covers all of your requirements.
- Pay close attention to the tiny print.
- Make certain that you understand the policy's exclusions and restrictions.

Are you planning a vacation to Laos? Here are some visa and currency conversion tips:

- If eligible, get a visa on arrival.
- Currency exchange can be done at a bank or money exchange agency.
- Credit cards and abms should be used with prudence.
- Purchase travel insurance.

You can simply manage the visa and currency exchange processes in Laos and have a seamless vacation with a little forethought.

Travel Insurance for Laos

Laos is a lovely nation with plenty to offer visitors. Laos has something for everyone, from the breathtaking scenery of the Mekong River to the ancient temples of Luang Prabang. However, there are hazards associated with any trip location. That is why having travel insurance is essential when visiting Laos. Travel insurance can help you financially safeguard yourself in the case of an accident, sickness, or other unanticipated incident. It can also assist in paying for lost or damaged bags, missing flights, and other travel inconveniences. There are several travel insurance products available, therefore it is critical to look around and compare coverage before purchasing. <u>When selecting a travel insurance coverage, keep the following aspects in mind:</u>

- The amount of coverage you require: Some insurance provide only basic coverage, while others provide more extensive coverage. Consider the activities you want to undertake in Laos and ensure that your insurance coverage covers you for any potential dangers.
- The deductible is as follows: The deductible is the amount you must pay out of pocket before your insurance coverage takes effect. Choose a coverage with a manageable deductible.
- The maximum payment is as follows: The maximum payment is the most money your insurance provider will pay you if you file a claim. Choose a policy with a high enough maximum payment to cover your probable losses.
- The waiting period: Some plans contain a waiting period, which is the amount of time you must wait before filing a claim. If feasible, select a policy with a short waiting time.
- Once you've decided on travel insurance coverage, make sure you read the tiny print and

understand the terms and conditions. You should also have your insurance papers with you on your vacation.

Here are some more suggestions for making the most of your travel insurance:

- Check that your insurance coverage covers COVID-19: COVID-19 is a big worry for 2024 travelers. Check to see if your coverage covers the cost of medical care, quarantine, and any related costs.
- Purchase travel insurance as soon as you schedule your vacation: Travel insurance is often less expensive if purchased sooner rather than later.
- Inform your insurance company of any pre-existing conditions: If you have any pre-existing ailments, notify your insurance carrier. This will assist in guaranteeing that your coverage covers any connected costs.

- Keep the following policy papers with you on your trip: In the case of a claim, you must produce your policy documents to your insurance carrier.
- Travel insurance is an essential component of any trip to Laos. You may assist in protecting yourself financially in the case of an accident, sickness, or other unanticipated disaster by taking the time to select the correct insurance and understand the terms and conditions.

In 2024, the following are some of the top travel insurance providers for Laos:

World Nomads: World Nomads is a popular option for Laos travelers. They provide a variety of coverage alternatives and their plans are simple to read.

Travel Guard: This is yet another well-known travel insurance provider. They provide a range of coverage choices and provide good customer service.

AIG Travel Insurance: AIG is a large insurance firm that provides travel insurance. Their policies are extensive, and their customer service is excellent.

Whatever travel insurance provider you pick, make sure you thoroughly read the tiny print and understand the terms and conditions of your coverage. This ensures that you are protected in the case of an accident, sickness, or other unanticipated incident.

Where Can I Get Laos Travel Insurance?

Travel insurance for Laos is available from a variety of providers, including:

- Your travel agent's name is: As part of their services, several travel agencies provide travel insurance.
- Purchase travel insurance directly from an insurance company: You may also purchase travel insurance straight from an insurance company.

- There are several websites that provide travel insurance.

Tips for Purchasing Laos Travel Insurance

Here are some pointers for purchasing Laos travel insurance:

- Look around. Before purchasing coverage, compare rates from other insurance providers.
- Purchase your coverage in advance. You will not be able to purchase travel insurance after you are in Laos.
- Read the policy thoroughly. Before you acquire insurance, be sure you understand all of the terms and conditions.
- Keep your policy information close at hand. If you file a claim, you may be required to disclose your policy information to your insurance carrier.

Travel insurance is an essential component of any trip to Laos. It can assist protect you financially in the event of a medical emergency, travel cancellation, or other unanticipated situations. When purchasing Laos travel insurance, check rates from many insurance firms and thoroughly study the policy before purchasing.

Booking your flights and accommodation

- Choose your trip dates. Laos is a year-round destination, but the dry season, which runs from November to March, is the greatest time to visit. During this period, the weather is nice, with typical temperatures ranging from 25 to 30 degrees Celsius.
- Determine your budget. The cost of accommodation in Laos may range from cheap hostels to expensive resorts. Set a budget before you begin arranging your vacation to ensure that you do not overpay.

- Select your destination. Laos has a diverse range of places, each with its own distinct personality. Popular tourist sites include Luang Prabang, Vientiane, Vang Vieng, and Pakse.
- Plan your flights. Because there are no direct flights from most major cities to Laos, you will most likely need to make at least one connection. There are several airlines that travel to Laos, so make sure to research fares before booking your ticket.
- Make a reservation for your lodging. Laos has a wide range of housing alternatives, from hostels to luxury hotels. It is important to reserve your accommodations ahead of time, especially if you are traveling during high season.
- Obtain your visa. To enter Laos, citizens of the majority of nations must apply for a visa. A visa can be obtained online or at the Laotian embassy or consulate in your own country.
- Pack your belongings and begin organizing your journey! Laos is a lovely nation with plenty to

offer visitors. You may enjoy an amazing trip with proper planning.

Here are some extra suggestions for arranging flights and lodging in Laos:

- Be flexible with your trip dates. If your vacation dates are flexible, you may be able to discover better discounts on flights and lodging.
- Travel during the shoulder seasons (April to June or September to October). During these months, the weather remains beautiful, but costs are often cheaper.
- Plan ahead of time for your flights and accommodations, especially if you're traveling during high season (November to March).
- Consider purchasing a package deal that includes your flights and lodging. Package offers may frequently help you save money.
- Before making a reservation, read reviews of various lodging alternatives. This will assist you

in selecting the best alternative for your requirements.
- Before you book, compare costs from several airlines and lodging providers. This will assist you in locating the greatest offers.

When making your budget, remember to include the costs of transportation, food, and activities.

Health and Safety in Laos

Laos is a safe nation for visitors to visit, having a low crime rate. There are, however, a few health and safety concerns that visitors should be aware of.

Diarrhea

Diarrhea is a common complaint among Laotian visitors, and it can be caused by a number of circumstances, including contaminated food and water, climatic changes, and stress. Diarrhea symptoms include stomach cramping, loose feces, and dehydration. If you have diarrhea, you should drink plenty of water and consume bland meals. To assist in easing symptoms, you may also choose to use over-the-counter medicine.

Malaria

Malaria is a mosquito-borne disease that, if untreated, can be lethal. Malaria is a danger in Laos, particularly in rural regions. It is critical to use insect repellent, wear long sleeves and pants, and sleep under a mosquito net to protect yourself against malaria. You should also think about taking malaria treatment before your trip.

High-altitude illness

Laos is a hilly nation, and travelers who rise to high heights too rapidly risk altitude sickness. Altitude sickness symptoms include headache, nausea, vomiting, dizziness, and exhaustion. If you notice any of these symptoms, you should descend to a lower altitude as quickly as possible.

Traffic safety

Road conditions in Laos can be poor, and traffic accidents are common. It is critical to drive slowly and cautiously, keeping an eye out for pedestrians and other cars. You should also always use a seatbelt.

Wildlife

Snakes, spiders, and monkeys are among the natural species of Laos that might pose a hazard to humans. It is essential to be aware of these creatures and to take care to prevent coming into touch with them. If you are bitten by an animal, you should seek medical assistance right away.

Healthcare

Laos' healthcare system is not as developed as that of other nations. There are minimal resources, and wait periods might be lengthy. If you require medical assistance, it is critical that you carry travel insurance that includes medical evacuation.

Other dangers

Other dangers that travelers visiting Laos should be aware of are as follows:

Heatstroke: Because Laos may be hot and humid, staying hydrated and avoiding vigorous exercise during the warmest portions of the day are essential.

Snakebites: Snakes are plentiful in Laos, therefore be cautious when trekking or camping. If you are bitten by a snake, you should seek medical assistance right away.

Terrorism: Although there is minimal danger of terrorism in Laos, it is vital to be aware of the possibility. If you are planning a trip to Laos, you should check the security situation ahead of time.

You may assist in guaranteeing a safe and happy vacation to Laos by adopting a few basic steps.

Here are some more safety and health considerations for Laos:

- Consume safe food: Eat food that has been completely prepared and is served hot. Consume raw or undercooked meat, seafood, or eggs.
- Safe water to drink: Bottled water is widely accessible in Laos. Drinking tap water or ice cubes created from tap water is not recommended.
- Vaccinate yourself: Before traveling to Laos, make careful to be vaccinated against the following diseases: hepatitis A, typhoid, cholera, and yellow fever.
- To defend yourself against mosquitoes, use an insect repellent containing DEET.
- Be mindful of your surroundings: When walking or driving in Laos, be alert of your surroundings. Take extra precautions at night.
- Believe your instincts: If you feel dangerous in any scenario, believe your instincts and get out of there.

You may assist in guaranteeing a safe and pleasurable vacation to Laos by following these guidelines.

Copyrighted Material

Memories From My Laos Trip

Date: _____ Destination: _____

NOTE

CHAPTER 3

Getting Around Laos

Getting around Laos as a visitor in 2024 will be an adventure in and of itself. Laos offers a diversified transportation network that allows tourists to discover its treasures, from bustling metropolises to isolated villages. In this guide, we will look at the various kinds of transportation accessible and offer advice on how to get around Laos efficiently.

Domestic Flights in Laos

In Laos, there are two domestic airlines: Lao Airlines and Lao Skyway. Lao Airlines is the country's flag airline, and it serves more destinations than Lao Skyway. Lao Skyway is a tiny airline that offers lower-cost flights to popular locations.

Which Airlines Operate in Laos?

Lao Airlines: Lao Airlines is the country's flag carrier, and it serves more destinations than Lao Skyway. The airline's fleet consists of Airbus A320, ATR 72-500, and ATR 72-600 planes.

Lao Skyway: This is a minor airline that provides more cheap flights to certain popular locations. The airline's fleet consists of Cessna 208 Grand Caravan and MA-60 planes.

Why Should You Book Laos Domestic Flights?

There are several reasons why you should plan domestic flights in Laos:

- To save time: If you are going between far Laos destinations, domestic flights might save you a lot of time. For example, driving from Vientiane to Luang Prabang might take up to 12 hours, whereas flying takes only an hour.
- To avoid the trouble of border crossings: If you are traveling between Laos and another nation, you will need to cross a border. This may be a

lengthy and complicated procedure. Domestic flights might spare you the trouble of crossing borders.
- To learn about Laos' many cultures: Laos is a diversified country with a rich culture. Domestic flights allow you to discover the many cultures of Laos in different sections of the nation.

Which Laos Airlines Have the Best Domestic Flight Deals?

Throughout the year, both Lao Airlines and Lao Skyway offer domestic flight bargains. The finest bargains, however, are generally available during the low season (May-October). Domestic flight bargains may be found by visiting airline websites or utilizing a flight search engine.

How Much Does a Domestic Flight in Laos Cost?

Domestic flight prices in Laos vary based on the route, carrier, and time of year.

Here is an example of Laos domestic flight fares in 2024:

- USD 100-150 from Vientiane to Luang Prabang
- USD 150-200 from Vientiane to Pakse.
- USD 100-150 from Vientiane to Savannakhet
- USD 150-200 from Vientiane to Oudomxay
- USD 150-200 from Luang Prabang to Pakse
- USD 100-150 from Luang Prabang to Savannakhet
- USD 150-200 from Luang Prabang to Oudomxay
- USD 50-100 from Pakse to Savannakhet
- USD 100-150 from Pakse to Oudomxay; USD 50-100 from Savannakhet to Oudomxay

If you intend to fly within Laos, it is recommended to purchase your tickets ahead of time, especially during the high tourist season. Tickets can be purchased online or through a travel agency. Check the luggage allowance before buying your flights. For internal flights, both Lao Airlines and Lao Skyway allow 20kg of luggage.

Domestic flights in Laos are a simple method to travel within the nation. They are also an excellent choice if you are short on time. However, they may be costly, so book your tickets ahead of time and double-check the luggage allowance.

How to Find Low-Cost Domestic Flights in Laos

- Purchase your tickets in advance.
- Travel dates should be flexible.
- Consider traveling with a smaller airline like Lao Skyway.
- Fly between the months of March and May, and September and October.
- Look for exclusive offers and promotions.
- Register for email updates from airlines.

Domestic flights in Laos may be a quick and effective method to travel across the nation. They can, however, be pricey, so do your homework and book your tickets ahead of time.

You can locate inexpensive domestic flights in Laos and save money on your next trip by using the recommendations provided above.

Buses in Laos

Buses are a common means of transportation in Laos, particularly for long-distance travel. There are several bus companies to select from, each with its own set of services and costs.

As a traveler to Laos in 2024, here's what you need to know about buses:

- Buses are classified into two sorts in Laos: public buses and private minivans. The cheapest choice is public transportation, although it may be sluggish and busy. Private minivans are more costly, but they are more comfortable and speedier.
- Prices vary based on the distance traveled and the kind of bus used in Laos. An average public bus

trip from Vientiane to Luang Prabang is roughly $10. A private minivan will cost roughly $20 from Vientiane to Luang Prabang.

- Bus timetables in Laos differ based on the provider. Most buses, however, leave large cities in the morning and evening.
- Bus tickets may be purchased in advance at bus stops or online. It is best to get tickets in advance, especially during peak season.
- What to expect: Most buses in Laos are not air-conditioned. Prepare for hot and humid weather, especially during the summer.
- Safety: Laos buses are typically safe. It is, nonetheless, prudent to be aware of your surroundings and to take safeguards against petty theft.

Here are some guidelines for visiting Laos and traveling buses:

- Purchase your tickets in advance to ensure that you receive a seat on the bus of your choice.

- Arrive early at the bus terminal to provide time to purchase your ticket, locate your bus, and settle in.
- Bring snacks and drinks: Laos buses do not provide food or beverages, so bring your own.
- Prepare for a bumpy trip: The roads in Laos may be rocky, so plan for a bumpy ride.
- Keep an eye on your surroundings: Keep your valuables close at hand and be on the lookout for any unusual activities.

Overall, buses are a safe and inexpensive method to go about Laos. You may ensure a pleasant and pleasurable travel by following these recommendations.

Here are some more details about buses in Laos in 2024:

- The Laotian government has donated 600 new buses to the country's public transportation system. These buses are more pleasant for passengers since they have air conditioning and other amenities.

- Road improvements: The Laotian government is also investing in the country's road network. This will improve the efficiency and dependability of bus travel.
- Increased demand: Laos's expanding tourist industry is also leading to an increase in demand for bus travel. People are increasingly opting to travel by bus to see the country's various attractions.

Buses are becoming an increasingly popular means of transportation in Laos as a result of these causes. If you're thinking of visiting Laos in 2024, consider riding the bus. It is a safe, inexpensive, and convenient method to travel across the country.

Trains in Laos

The train is one of the greatest ways to see Laos. The country's railway network is modest, but it is well-maintained and efficient.

The trains are luxurious and provide breathtaking views of the surrounding landscape.

In Laos, there are two major railroad routes:

The Vientiane-Luang Prabang line: This is Laos' most popular train route. The drive takes around 12 hours and travels through some of the most magnificent landscapes in the nation, including the Vang Vieng Karst mountains.
The Vientiane-Boten line: This is Laos's newest railroad route. The drive takes around 8 hours and takes you through northern Laos' highlands and valleys.

Laos train tickets are reasonably priced. A one-way trip from Vientiane to Luang Prabang is around $20, while a ticket from Vientiane to Boten is about $30.

Here are some pointers about traveling by rail in Laos:

- Plan ahead of time, especially if you're traveling during the high season.

- Arrive at the railway station 30 minutes before your scheduled departure time.
- Bring your passport and visa with you in case the ticket inspector needs them.
- Wear comfortable clothing and shoes because you may be walking around the railway terminals.
- Bring snacks and beverages with you because train meals and drinks may be costly.
- Enjoy the journey and the breathtaking sights!

<u>*Here are some of the advantages and disadvantages of traveling the train in Laos:*</u>

Pros:

- Trains are a convenient and cost-effective mode of transportation in Laos.
- Trains provide spectacular views over the surrounding area.
- Train tickets are reasonably priced.

Cons:

- Laos' railroad network is rather tiny, hence there are few alternatives for travel.
- Trains may be sluggish, especially on the route from Vientiane to Boten.
- Because there aren't many amenities on the trains, you'll need to carry your own food and beverages.

Overall, using the train in Laos is an excellent way to explore the country. It is a convenient and fast mode of transportation that provides breathtaking views of the surrounding landscape. If you're going to Laos, I strongly recommend riding the train!

Boats in Laos

In Laos, there are many distinct types of boats, each with its own set of pros and limitations. A small motorboat or longtail boat is a nice alternative for short journeys, such as a day trip to a local hamlet. These boats are reasonably priced to hire and can readily handle tight canals and rivers.

A bigger boat with overnight lodging is a preferable alternative for longer voyages, such as the one from Luang Prabang to Vientiane. These boats give additional comfort and room, as well as food and other amenities. The slow boat from Huay Xai to Luang Prabang is one of the most popular boat journeys in Laos. This two-day trek down the Mekong River provides breathtaking views of the surrounding landscape. The slow boat is a terrific way to relax and take in the sights, and it is far less expensive than flying or taking the bus.

The journey from Vientiane to Pakse is another popular boat tour. This four-day trek follows the Mekong River and stops at several intriguing locations, including the Pak Ou Caves and the Bolaven Plateau. The trip is a more luxurious choice than the slow boat for seeing a lot of Laos in a short length of time.

Whatever style of boat tour you pick, you will have a fantastic time in Laos. Boats are an excellent opportunity to see the nation and experience its distinct culture.

Here is a list of some of Laos' most popular boat excursions:

Slow Boat from Thailand to Laos: A two-day cruise on the Mekong River from Huay Xai, Thailand to Luang Prabang, Laos. The boat makes many stops along the trip, allowing passengers to explore rural Laos. The slow boat pricing varies, but it is usually approximately $150 for two persons.

The Luang Say trip: This is a three-day Mekong River trip from Luang Prabang to Pakbeng. The trip makes numerous stops along the route and includes a visit to the Pak Ou Caves. The cost of the Luang Say Cruise varies, but for two persons, it is normally approximately $300.

The Mekong River Boat Tour: This is a one-day Mekong River cruise from Luang Prabang. The excursion includes a visit to a local village, a stop at a floating market, and the opportunity to observe some of the Mekong River's animals. The Mekong River Boat Tour pricing varies, but it is usually approximately $50 for two persons.

Vang Vieng Cave Tubing: This is a one-day adventure that involves floating down a river through a succession of caverns. The caverns are illuminated with colorful lights, making the experience both thrilling and soothing. The cost of cave tubing in Vang Vieng varies, but it is usually approximately $30 per person.

The Pha That Luang excursion: This is a one-hour Mekong River excursion from Vientiane. The boat passes by Pha That Luang, one of Laos' most recognized attractions. The Pha That Luang Cruise pricing varies, but it is usually approximately $10 for two persons.

These are just a handful of the many boat trips offered in Laos. Boats can be found to meet visitors' budgets and interests.

<u>Here are some extra boating advice for Laos:</u>

- Pre-book your boat: This is especially necessary during peak season (November to March).
- Dress appropriately: Wear comfortable clothing and shoes suited for the weather.
- Bring a hat and sunscreen: The sun may be very intense in Laos, thus it is essential to protect oneself from its rays.
- Bring a camera: You'll want to document all of your boating moments.
- Respect the locals: Because Laos is a Buddhist nation, you should respect the locals and their customs.

- Taking a boat in Laos is an excellent opportunity to discover the country's natural beauty and rich culture. With so many different boat experiences to select from, you're bound to find one that's ideal for you.

Here are some examples of boat trip pricing in Laos in 2024:

- Slow boat from Huay Xai to Luang Prabang costs between $50 and $100 per person.
- The cost of a cruise from Vientiane to Pakse is between $200 and $400 per person.
- A motorboat or longtail boat for a day excursion costs between $20 and $50.
- Larger boats with overnight accommodations cost between $100 and $200 per passenger per night.

Taxis and Tuk-Tuks in Laos

Taxis and tuk-tuks are two of the most common modes of transportation in Laos. They are both reasonably priced and can be obtained in most major cities and tourist areas.

Taxis

Taxis in Laos are metered, so you can be certain of the fare before you begin your journey. The basic fee is usually approximately 2000 kip (US$0.20), and the pricing per kilometer varies by city. In Vientiane, for example, the charge is 300 kip (US$0.03) per km, whereas in Luang Prabang, the rate is 400 kip (US$0.04) per kilometer. Taxis are typically trustworthy and safe, but there are a few things to be careful of. To begin, ensure that the taxi is metered. If it isn't, haggle the fare before you board. Second, be aware that certain taxi drivers, especially if you are a tourist, may try to overcharge you. If you are unsure about the fare, request that the driver show you the meter.

Tuk-tuks

Tuk-tuks are three-wheeled motorcycle-powered vehicles. They are not metered, therefore you must bargain the fee with the driver before getting in. Tuk-tuks are a popular mode of transportation in Laos because they are affordable and can readily weave through traffic. However, there are a few things to keep in mind while taking a tuk-tuk. Before you get in, be sure you and the driver have agreed on a fare. Second, be willing to bargain. Tuk-tuk drivers sometimes start with a high charge, so be prepared to bargain. Third, be aware that tuk-tuks are not necessarily the safest mode of transportation. They may be overcrowded, and the drivers may be inexperienced.

Which is superior? Tuk-tuks or taxis?

There is no simple answer to whether cabs or tuk-tuks are superior. Both have their own set of benefits and drawbacks. Taxis are more dependable and secure, but they might be more costly. Tuk-tuks are less priced, but they are not guaranteed to be as trustworthy or safe.

Finally, deciding which method of transportation is suitable for you is the best approach to travel around in Laos. Taxis are the best alternative for a dependable and safe mode of transportation. Tuk-tuks are a better alternative if you're searching for a cheap method to travel about.

Here is a table with approximate taxi and tuk-tuk prices in several of Laos' major cities:

- Taxi fare in the city the cost of a tuk-tuk ride
- Vientiane 2000 km/h1000 kip/km
- Luang Prabang is a city in Laos.3000 kip/km2000 kip/km
- Pakse4000 kip/km2500 kip/km
- Savannakhet 5000 km/h3000 kip/km

Taxis and tuk-tuks in Laos: *Here are some pointers.*

- Always haggle the cost before boarding.
- Keep an eye on your surroundings and take care to avoid theft.
- If you are not comfortable with the driver, request that they pull over and let you out.
- Trust your instincts. If something does not feel right, it most likely is not.

Rental Cars in Laos

Driving is one of the greatest ways to see Laos. Rental automobiles are widely accessible in all major cities, and the costs are reasonable. *The following is a breakdown of the average automobile rental pricing in Laos in 2024:*

- $35 per day for an economy vehicle
- $42 per day for a compact vehicle
- Intermediate automobile rental is $55 per day.
- Full-size automobile rental is $75 per day.
- $82 per day for an SUV

Prices for renting a car in Laos vary based on the time of year, the type of vehicle rented, and the rental business used. Booking your rental car ahead of time is always a smart idea, especially during high season.

There are a few factors to bear in mind while hiring a car in Laos:

- A valid driver's license from your native country is required.
- To hire a car in Laos, you must be at least 21 years old.
- Additional insurance, such as collision damage waiver (CDW) and theft protection, may be necessary.
- In Laos, the speed limit in cities is 60 kilometers per hour (37 miles per hour), whereas on highways it is 80 kilometers per hour (50 miles per hour).
- Driving under the influence of alcohol is banned in Laos.

Renting a car in Laos allows you to explore the nation at your leisure. With so many low-cost alternatives available, you may choose the ideal vehicle for your needs and budget.

Here are some recommendations for hiring a car in Laos:

- Pre-book your rental car, especially during high season.
- Prices from various rental businesses should be compared.
- Before signing the rental agreement, thoroughly read everything.
- Understand the local traffic rules and regulations.
- Drive conservatively and expect the unexpected.

Renting a car in Laos may be a safe and pleasurable experience with a little forethought.

Here are some more things to think about while hiring a car in Laos:

- Because the roads in Laos can be harsh, it is important to purchase a car in decent condition.
- Laos' highways include a lot of tolls, so be prepared to pay for them.
- If you intend to drive to a distant location, be sure you have a decent map and a full tank of petrol.
- Keep an eye out for wildlife on the roadways, especially in the early morning and late evening.

Renting a car in Laos is a terrific way to see the country, but be prepared for the difficulties that come with driving in a developing nation. By following these guidelines, you may ensure a safe and pleasurable rental vehicle experience in Laos.

CHAPTER 4

Things to Do in Laos

As a tourist in 2024, you'll be able to discover stunning landscapes, immerse yourself in historic customs, and savor delectable food. This guide will showcase some of the best things to do in Laos, as well as pricing information to help you plan your trip successfully.

Luang Prabang

Luang Prabang, Laos, is a lovely city recognized for its UNESCO World Heritage Site classification, French colonial architecture, and rich Buddhist heritage. For good reason, it is a popular tourist attraction. In Luang Prabang, there is plenty to see and do, from touring temples and palaces to trekking in the nearby mountains.

If you're thinking of visiting Luang Prabang in 2024, here's a rundown of what you can do and how much it will cost:

Visit the World Heritage Site designated by UNESCO. Luang Prabang's UNESCO World Heritage Site includes a collection of temples, palaces, and other ancient structures. The admission price is 20,000 Kip (US$1.05).

Go trekking in the nearby mountains. In the highlands around Luang Prabang, there are several hiking paths. A guided hike costs different amounts based on the duration of the trek and the number of persons in your party.

Attend a culinary lesson. In Luang Prabang, there are several culinary schools available. The cost of a cooking class varies according to the length of the class and the type of cuisine that will be prepared.

Visit a nearby market. In Luang Prabang, there are several local markets where you can buy souvenirs, handicrafts, and fresh fruit. The market price of products changes based on the item.

Spend the day in a spa. In Luang Prabang, there are several spas where you may have a massage, facial, or other spa service. The cost of spa treatments varies based on the type of therapy and its duration.

Take a boat ride along the Mekong River. There are several boat cruises available on the Mekong River. A boat journey's cost varies according to the duration of the trip and the kind of boat.

Take pleasure in a typical Laotian dinner. Traditional Laotian cuisine is available at a variety of restaurants in Luang Prabang. A lunch in a restaurant costs different amounts based on the type of food and the location of the establishment.

These are just a handful of the various activities available in Luang Prabang. Whatever your hobbies are, you will find something to enjoy in this lovely city.

When to go: The dry season, which spans from November to April, is the finest time to explore Luang Prabang. The weather is pleasant and bright, with minimal chance of rain.

However, the dry season is also the most busy, so if you prefer a more serene experience, consider going during the rainy season, which runs from May to October.

Getting there: Flying is the most convenient method to get to Luang Prabang. There are direct flights from both Vientiane, Laos' capital, and Bangkok, Thailand. You may take a taxi or tuk-tuk into the city center once you arrive at Luang Prabang Airport.

Where to stay: In Luang Prabang, there are several hotels and guesthouses to select from, ranging from budget-friendly alternatives to opulent resorts. If you're on a tight budget, I recommend staying in the historic district. This is where the majority of the attractions are, as well as the most atmospheric area of the city.

The following is a breakdown of some of the average costs in Luang Prabang in 2024:

Accommodation: A dorm bed at a hostel costs between $5 and $10 per night. A modest hotel room costs between $15 and $20 per night. A mid-range hotel room costs between $30 and $50 per night. A deluxe hotel room might cost more than $100 per night.

Food: A lunch at a street food stand will cost you around US$1-2. A lunch at a neighborhood eatery will cost you about US$3-5. A dinner in a mid-range restaurant costs between $10 and $15 USD. A lunch at a high-end restaurant will set you back at least $20.

Beverages: A beer costs about US$1-2. A glass of wine costs between $3 and $5 USD. A drink costs between $5 and $10 USD.

Activities: The UNESCO World Heritage Site has an admission cost of 20,000 Kip (US$1.05). A guided trek costs between $10 and $20 USD. A culinary session will cost you between $20 and $30. A trip to the local market costs about $5. A day at the spa costs between $50 and $100. A boat excursion on the Mekong River costs between $10 and $20 USD.

Overall, Luang Prabang is an inexpensive place to visit. You can easily locate affordable lodging, food, and recreational activities.

Vientiane

Vientiane, Laos' capital, is a city of contrasts. Its inhabitants are a blend of traditional Lao and global cultures, and it is home to both old temples and contemporary skyscrapers. Visitors will find Vientiane to be both pleasant and lively, offering something for everyone. Wandering through Vientiane's streets and marketplaces is one of the greatest ways to get to know the city. The city is teeming with brightly colored stores and kiosks offering everything from souvenirs to fresh fruit. Make sure to bargain for the best deal! Visit some of Vientiane's many temples if you're interested in history and culture. Wat Sisaket, which was established in the 18th century and includes a collection of Buddha statues, is the most well-known. Wat Ho Pha Bang, Wat Xieng Thong, and Wat That Luang are among the other prominent temples.

If you want to do something more active, Vientiane has lots of options. You may stroll or bike along the Mekong River, or take a boat tour to one of the river's numerous islands. There are also a number of parks and gardens across the city where you can unwind and take in the view. Vientiane comes alive at night with a thriving entertainment scene. Traditional Lao pubs to fashionable Western-style bars cater to a wide range of tastes. Try some of the native cuisine, which is among the greatest in Southeast Asia.

Vientiane is a wonderful location to unwind and relax, but it is also a vibrant city with much to offer tourists. Whether you like history, culture, nature, or nightlife, Vientiane has something for everyone.

The following is a proposed itinerary for a three-day visit to Vientiane:

Day 1:

- Visit Wat Sisaket and Wat Ho Pha Bang in the morning.
- Afternoon: Take a Mekong River boat ride.
- Evening: Go shopping at the night markets.

Day 2:

- Visit Wat Xieng Thong and Wat That Luang in the morning.
- In the afternoon, unwind in one of Vientiane's many parks or gardens.
- Evening: Dine at a local restaurant on a typical Lao dinner.

Day 3:

- Visit the Lao National Museum in the morning.
- Afternoon: Enroll in a culinary class.
- Evening: Attend a show at the Pha That Luang National Theatre.

Of course, this is only a suggestion; you may modify your schedule to your own interests. You'll have a wonderful experience in Vientiane no matter how you spend your time there.

Here are some other suggestions to help you plan your vacation to Vientiane:

- The dry season, which lasts from November to April, is the greatest time to visit Vientiane.
- Laos' official currency is the kip. US currencies, on the other hand, are frequently accepted in Vientiane.
- Tipping is not customary in Laos.
- Lao is the official language of Laos. English, on the other hand, is commonly spoken in Vientiane.
- In Vientiane, there are a variety of decent hotels to suit all budgets.

Vang Vieng

Vang Vieng is a tiny town in central Laos that has undergone significant change in recent years. Vang Vieng, once known as a backpacker party town, is now a magnet for outdoor enthusiasts and environmental lovers. The village is set in a valley surrounded by karst mountains. The environment is breathtaking, and there are numerous hiking, biking, kayaking, and rock climbing activities. Tham Chang, a big cave with magnificent limestone structures, is one of numerous caves to explore. Vang Vieng is also a wonderful spot to unwind and enjoy the relaxed atmosphere. There are several restaurants and pubs to pick from, and the people are warm and pleasant. If you want to have an experience in gorgeous surroundings, Vang Vieng is the place to be.

A 5-day journey to Vang Vieng in 2024 may look like this:

Day 1: Arrive in Vang Vieng and settle into your accommodation. Spend the afternoon visiting the town and getting to know it. Enjoy a welcome supper at a local restaurant in the evening.

Day 2: Take a trek or a bike ride in the nearby countryside. Take a kayak cruise on the Nam Song River in the afternoon. In the evening, unwind at a local pub or treat yourself to a traditional Laotian massage.

Day 3: Explore the limestone structures of Tham Chang Cave. Go rock climbing or whitewater rafting in the afternoon. In the evening, gather your friends for a campfire and a BBQ.

Day 4: Spend the day exploring the Pak Ou caves, which are approximately an hour's drive from Vang Vieng. Visit the Phu Hin Bun National Protected Area in the afternoon and go for a trek in the jungle. Enjoy a goodbye supper at a local restaurant in the evening.

Day 5: Unwind at the pool or beach before departing. Take a cooking class or learn about Laotian culture in the afternoon. Enjoy a goodbye meal at your hotel in the evening.

Of course, this is only a recommended schedule; you may modify it to your own interests and tastes. There are many other things to see and do in Vang Vieng, so no matter what you do, you'll have a fantastic day.

Here are some other suggestions to help you plan your vacation to Vang Vieng:

- The dry season, which lasts from November to April, is the best time to visit Vang Vieng.
- Vang Vieng has a wide range of housing alternatives, so you can find something to suit your needs.
- When shopping in Vang Vieng, remember to haggle. Prices for visitors are frequently jacked up.
- Tipping is not expected, but it is valued in Laos.

- Before you leave, learn some fundamental Laotian phrases. This will improve your communication skills and make your journey more pleasurable.

Si Phan Don (Four Thousand Islands),

Si Phan Don, popularly known as the 4,000 Islands, is a riverine archipelago in Champasak Province, southern Laos, on the Mekong River. With lush rainforests, towering limestone cliffs, and crystal-clear waterways, it is a really wonderful spot. The islands are home to several ethnic groups, each with its own distinct culture and customs.

In 2023, I went to Si Phan Don, and it was one of the most amazing experiences of my life. My days were spent swimming, kayaking, hiking, and exploring the islands. I also met some incredible people from all around the world.

Here are some of my favorite aspects of Si Phan Don:

The natural beauty of the islands is breathtaking. The Mekong River is a lovely river, with thick forests and high limestone cliffs that encircle the islands.

The relaxed atmosphere: Si Phan Don is a very relaxed environment. Because the islands have no vehicles or motorcycles, the only way to get about is by foot, bicycle, or boat. This results in a very serene and pleasant environment.

Folks are friendly: The folks of Si Phan Don are among the nicest I've ever encountered. They are constantly keen to share their culture and customs with visitors and are always pleased to assist them.

There are several activities to choose from in Si Phan Don. Swimming, kayaking, hiking, exploring the islands, visiting communities, and learning about the local culture are all options. Si Phan Don has something for everyone. I definitely recommend visiting Si Phan Don if you want a genuinely amazing trip experience. It's a genuinely lovely spot, and I'm sure you'll like it.

Here are some pointers to help you organize your vacation to Si Phan Don:

- The dry season, from November to April, is the optimum time to visit Si Phan Don. The weather is pleasant and bright, and the water levels are low, making exploration of the islands simpler.
- There are several ways to go to Si Phan Don. You may fly to Pakse, the provincial capital, and then take a bus or minivan to Ban Nakasang. You may take a boat from Ban Nakasang to one of the islands. A boat may also be taken from Kratie, Cambodia, to Don Det.
- On the islands, there are a range of hotel alternatives. There are guesthouses, bungalows, and homestays to select from.
- The islands include a variety of eateries that serve both Lao and foreign cuisine.

When buying on the islands, remember to haggle. Prices for visitors are frequently exaggerated.

Traveling in Si Phan Don is really secure. However, being aware of your surroundings and taking measures against theft is always a smart idea.

Thakhek

Thakhek is a tiny city in Laos that is rapidly gaining popularity as a tourist attraction. It is around 300 km south of Vientiane in the Khammouane province. Thakhek is well-known for its gorgeous surroundings, kind people, and relaxed attitude.

Here are some things to look forward to if you visit Thakhek in 2024:

- Thakhek's weather is often hot and humid, with average temperatures ranging from 25 to 35 degrees Celsius. The rainy season lasts from May to October, however, rain can fall at any time of year.

- Thakhek is surrounded by breathtaking nature, including mountains, rivers, and waterfalls. There are several hiking, biking, and paddling options.
- The residents of Thakhek are recognized for their friendliness and hospitality. They are always willing to assist travelers and make them feel at ease.
- The ambiance: Thakhek offers a laid-back and calm ambiance. There is no hurry and bustle, and everyone is content to take their time.

Here are some of the activities available in Thakhek:

Visit the Thakhek Caverns: The Thakhek Caves are a collection of limestone caverns just outside of town. They are home to many different kinds of stalactites and stalagmites, as well as bats and other fauna.

Take a Mekong River boat ride: The Mekong River is an important river that runs through Thakhek. There are several chances for riverboat rides, which are a terrific way to observe the surrounding area.

Hike in the Phu Hin Bun National Park: About 30 km from Thakhek is the Phu Hin Bun National Park. It has a number of hiking paths, as well as waterfalls and caves.

Discover the local culture: Thakhek is home to a number of ethnic groups, each with its own distinct culture. There are several ways to learn about the local culture, such as visiting villages or attending cultural performances.

Relax on the beach: Because Thakhek is located on the banks of the Mekong River, there are several options to relax on the beach. There are a few swimming holes in the neighborhood as well, which are ideal for cooling down on a hot day.

Thakhek is an excellent choice for a relaxed and picturesque vacation in Laos. Thakhek, with its nice people, stunning environment, and laid-back culture, will make your trip to Laos unforgettable.

Here are some more suggestions for organizing a vacation to Thakhek in 2024:

- The dry season, which lasts from November to April, is the greatest time to visit Thakhek.
- If you intend to go hiking or riding, make sure to have lots of water and sunscreen.
- Thakhek offers a wide range of lodging alternatives, from budget-friendly guesthouses to luxury hotels.
- The Lao kip is the native currency.
- Thakhek is a generally safe city, although keep the normal precautions against petty theft in mind.

Pakse

Pakse is the capital of the Champasak province in southern Laos. It is situated on the Mekong River's banks, approximately 200 km from the Cambodian border. Pakse is a key transit hub and a renowned tourist attraction.

Pakse is predicted to be a significant tourist attraction during Visit Laos Year in 2024. *The city has several attractions for visitors, including:*

- Pakse has a rich history and culture, including old temples and ruins as well as traditional villages. Through its museums and cultural attractions, visitors may learn about the city's rich history and culture.
- Pakse is surrounded by a breathtaking natural environment, including mountains, waterfalls, and woods. In the nearby area, visitors may go hiking, riding, or kayaking.
- Pakse has a thriving culinary scene, with restaurants providing Laotian, Thai, and other Asian cuisine. Fresh seafood, delectable curries, and other regional delicacies are available to visitors.
- Pakse residents are well-known for their friendliness and hospitality. This lovely city will make visitors feel at ease.

Here is a 5-day schedule for a visit to Pakse in 2024:

Day 1: Arrive in Pakse and settle into your accommodation. Visit the Wat Phu Champasak temple complex in the afternoon, which is around 15 km outside the city. In the evening, dine at a local restaurant for a traditional Laotian meal.

Day 2: Spend the day touring the historic town of Pakse. The Champasak National Museum, the Pakse Market, and the Pha That Luang temple are all worth seeing. Take a sunset boat trip down the Mekong River in the evening.

Day 3: Visit Vang Vieng, a picturesque village around 100 km from Pakse. Spend the day exploring the nearby countryside by hiking, biking, or kayaking. In the evening, dine at one of Vang Vieng's numerous eateries.

Day 4: Travel to the Bolaven Plateau, a hilly location roughly 200 km from Pakse. Spend the day hiking, riding, or exploring the local coffee farms.

In the evening, dine at a local restaurant for a traditional Laotian meal.

Day 5: Relax by your hotel pool or join a cooking lesson to learn how to create traditional Laotian meals. Enjoy a goodbye supper at a local restaurant in the evening.

Of course, this is only a recommended schedule; you may tailor it to your own interests and time limits. Pakse is a wonderful spot to unwind and explore, with something for everyone.

Here are some pointers to consider while considering a vacation to Pakse in 2024:

- Book your flights and accommodations early, especially if you're traveling during high season (November-December).
- Before you leave, learn some fundamental Laotian phrases.
- Bring comfortable shoes and attire for touring the city and its environs.

- Make sure to taste the local cuisine!
- Relax and enjoy your stay in this lovely city.

Champasak

Champasak is a little peaceful town in southern Laos well known as the entrance to the verdant and relaxed 4,000 Islands. Life here goes at a snail's pace (even by Lao standards), centered around rice harvests, coffee breaks, and the ebb and flow of the Mekong River.

In 2023, I visited Champasak and was instantly charmed by its beauty and tranquility. The village is on a bend in the Mekong River, with the magnificent remains of the Vat Phou temple rising in the background. Traditional Laotian dwellings line the streets, and the air is filled with the sound of songbirds.

My days were spent visiting the town and its surroundings. I went to Vat Phou, a UNESCO World Heritage Site, and was blown away by the beautiful carvings and sculptures.

In addition, I took a boat journey to the 4,000 Islands, where I spent my days swimming, kayaking, and trekking. Champasak appealed to me because of its relaxed attitude as well as its rich history and culture. It is the ideal location for getting away from the rush and bustle of everyday life and relaxing in the beauty of nature.

Here's a full report of my 2024 trip to Champasak:

Day 1: In the morning, I arrived in Champasak and booked into my hotel. I went for a walk around town after freshening up. I went to the market and got some souvenirs and food. I also went to a coffee shop to drink some coffee and watch people-watch.

Day 2: In the morning, I went to Vat Phou. Seeing this old structure up close was an incredible experience. I could have spent hours examining the ruins and marveling at the beautiful sculptures. I took a boat ride to Don Khon, one of the 4,000 Islands, in the afternoon.

The rest of the day was spent swimming, kayaking, and hiking.

Day 3: In the morning, I went to the Pakse Museum. It was fascinating to read about Champasak and the surrounding region's history. I attended a culinary lesson at a nearby restaurant in the afternoon. I learned how to cook some traditional Laotian foods, which I ate that night for supper.

Day 4: In the morning, I went to the Bolaven Plateau. The plateau is well-known for its beautiful scenery and coffee plantations. I spent the day hiking, riding, and seeing coffee plantations. I went on a boat ride on the Bolaven River in the afternoon.

Day 5: On my final day in Champasak, I relaxed by the pool at my hotel. I also got a massage and went souvenir shopping. I had a goodbye meal with my new pals in the evening.

I had a fantastic experience in Champasak. It is a lovely and serene setting, ideal for a relaxed holiday. I would strongly advise anyone searching for a one-of-a-kind and spectacular travel experience to visit Champasak.

Here are some pointers to help you organize your own vacation to Champasak:

- The dry season, which runs from November to April, is the best time to visit Champasak.
- There are several ways to get to Champasak. You may fly into Pakse International Airport or take a bus or rail from Vientiane.
- Champasak offers a wide range of hotel alternatives, from budget-friendly guest houses to upscale resorts.
- In Champasak, there are various things to see and do, such as visiting Vat Phou, seeing the 4,000 Islands, and trekking on the Bolaven Plateau.

Champasak is an excellent location for learning about Laotian culture and food. Try some of the local specialties, like laap, khao soi, and sticky rice.

Muang Ngoi Neua

Muang Ngoi Neua is a tiny hamlet in northern Laos located on the Nam Ou River's banks. It is a popular resort for tourists seeking a tranquil and pleasant getaway from the rush and bustle of metropolitan life. The settlement can only be reached by boat, adding to its impression of remoteness and isolation. When you arrive, you'll be met by traditional Laotian wooden buildings, tiny alleyways, and a few stores and restaurants. Muang Ngoi Neua has no vehicles or motorcycles, therefore the only way to get around is on foot or by bicycle. As a result, it is a very tranquil and quiet spot, ideal for lengthy walks or bike trips into the surrounding countryside. Relaxing and taking in the surroundings is one of the nicest things to do in Muang Ngoi Neua. The community is surrounded by mountains and thick forests, and the river views are truly breathtaking. There are also various caverns to explore, as well as climbing and trekking options. If you're searching for something to do in the evenings, the hamlet has a few restaurants and pubs where you can have a drink and some local cuisine. There is also a tiny cinema where movies are shown on a regular basis.

Muang Ngoi Neua is an excellent location for disconnecting from the worries of everyday life and reconnecting with nature. It is a genuinely one-of-a-kind and extraordinary site that will make an indelible impact on everybody who comes.

Here's a more thorough plan for a three-day journey to Muang Ngoi Neua:

Day 1: Arrive by boat at Muang Ngoi Neua and settle into your hotel. Spend the afternoon walking around the village's tiny streets and visiting the local stores and eateries. In the evening, dine at one of the restaurants that overlook the river.

Day 2: Hike to Tham Pha Tok, a big cave with beautiful views of the surrounding region, in the morning. In the afternoon, enjoy a bike ride through the countryside or a boat excursion down the Nam Ou River. In the evening, unwind at one of the village's pubs and share a drink with some new acquaintances.

Day 3: Visit the Pak Ou Caves in the morning, which house hundreds of Buddha sculptures. Take a cooking lesson in the afternoon and learn how to create some traditional Laotian cuisine. In the evening, have a goodbye meal at your favorite local restaurant.

Of course, this is only a suggestion; you may modify your schedule to your own interests. If you're searching for more excitement, you may go climbing or trekking in the nearby mountains, or you could even go whitewater rafting on the Nam Ou River. If you want to unwind, you may spend your days swimming in the river, reading a book in your hammock, or simply enjoying the peace and quiet of the town.

Whatever you do at Muang Ngoi Neua, you will have a remarkable experience. It's a wonderfully lovely spot that you'll remember long after you've left.

<u>Here are some other suggestions to help you organize your vacation to Muang Ngoi Neua:</u>

- The dry season, which runs from November to April, is the greatest time to visit.
- There are several ways to get to Muang Ngoi Neua. From Luang Prabang, you may take a bus or a boat to Nong Khiaw.
- Muang Ngoi Neua offers a wide range of hotel alternatives, from inexpensive guest houses to luxury resorts.
- Because the community is small and there aren't many stores or eateries, it's a good idea to pack some supplies.
- When shopping in the village, remember to haggle.
- Don't be hesitant to strike up a chat with the locals; they are incredibly polite and hospitable.

CHAPTER 5

Activities

Laos will not disappoint whether you are an adventurer, a history buff, or simply looking for a peaceful retreat. In this guide, we will look at some of the best things to do in Laos as a visitor.

Hiking and Trekking

In Laos, there are several hiking and trekking paths appropriate for all levels of expertise. *Among the most popular trails are:*

The Kuang Si Waterfall walk: A short and simple walk that leads to the breathtaking Kuang Si Waterfalls. The falls are around 30 km from Luang Prabang in the Phou Hin Namno National Protected Area.

The Nam Xay Viewpoint walk: This is a somewhat difficult walk that leads to the Nam Xay Viewpoint, which provides panoramic views of the surrounding landscape. The route is located around 100 km from Luang Prabang in the Nam Ha National Protected Area.

The Kuangsi Waterfall journey: This is a difficult three-day journey that goes to the Kuangsi Waterfalls. The falls are around 400 km from Luang Prabang in the Xe Pian National Protected Area.

The 100 Waterfalls journey: This is a difficult four-day journey that goes to 100 waterfalls. The hike takes place in southern Laos' Attapeu Province.

The Pha Daeng Peak trip: This is a difficult 5-day trip that leads to Pha Daeng Peak, Laos' highest mountain. The hike takes place in Phongsali Province in northern Laos.

In addition to these prominent routes, Laos has a plethora of additional hiking and trekking paths just waiting to be discovered. When climbing or trekking in Laos, it is critical to be weather prepared. Laos has a tropical environment with high humidity and warm temperatures. It is also critical to be ready for the terrain. Laos' routes may be difficult, with steep climbs and descents.

It is also critical to be aware of Laos' animals. Elephants, tigers, and bears are among the creatures found in the nation. When hiking or trekking in wildlife-infested areas, use extreme caution. Hiking and hiking in Laos are excellent ways to appreciate the country's natural splendour. It is also an excellent method to meet locals and learn about their culture. Hiking or trekking in Laos is an excellent alternative for those seeking excitement.

Here are some hiking and trekking advice for Laos:

- Hire a guide: A guide can assist you in planning your trip, locating the finest routes, and remaining safe.
- Prepare for the weather: The weather in Laos may be unpredictable, so pack for all possibilities.
- Prepare for the terrain: The trails in Laos may be difficult, so wear comfortable shoes and gear.

- Be mindful of wildlife: Laos is home to a wide range of animals, so be cautious when hiking or trekking in regions where wildlife is present.
- Bring plenty of water: Staying hydrated is essential whether hiking or trekking in Laos.
- Bring food: It is also a good idea to bring snacks with you on your trek in case you grow hungry.
- Respect the environment: Laos is a lovely nation, so please leave it as you found it.

Hiking and trekking in Laos are excellent ways to see the country's natural beauty and meet the locals. Hiking or trekking in Laos is an excellent alternative for those seeking excitement.

Kayaking and Rafting

Kayaking and rafting are two of the most popular outdoor sports among visitors visiting Laos. The area is home to a variety of rivers that offer beautiful scenery as well as difficult rapids, making it an ideal location for thrill seekers.

Laos is the place to go if you want a tough kayaking or rafting adventure. The Nam Ou River is a famous kayaking destination in Laos. It has a wide range of rapids ranging from Class II to Class IV, making it an excellent choice for experienced kayakers. The river also has several spectacular waterfalls, making it a gorgeous kayak.

If you want a more peaceful kayaking or rafting experience, Laos features a variety of rivers with softer rapids. The Mekong River is an excellent choice for novices. It has a range of rapids ranging from Class I to Class II, making it a safe and entertaining paddle for paddlers of all skill levels. The river is also home to several communities, making it an excellent chance to learn about local culture.

Whatever your skill level or experience, you'll discover a kayaking or rafting adventure in Laos that's suitable for you. *Here are some pointers to consider while arranging a kayaking or rafting excursion in Laos:*

- Choose the river that is appropriate for your ability level.
- Hire a knowledgeable tour guide.
- Bring the necessary equipment.
- Keep an eye on the weather forecast.
- Consider the environment.

You may enjoy a memorable kayaking or rafting trip in Laos with a little planning.

<u>Here are some of the top sites in Laos to go kayaking and rafting:</u>

Nam Ou River: Located in northern Laos, this river has a range of rapids ranging from Class II to Class IV. It's an excellent choice for seasoned kayakers.

Kayaking and rafting on the Nam Ou River in Laos

Mekong River: Located in central and southern Laos, this river has a range of rapids ranging from Class I to Class II. It's an excellent choice for both novice and experienced kayakers.

Nam Khan River: Located in Luang Prabang, this river has mild rapids and a wonderful landscape. It's an excellent option for families and beginners.

Kayaking and rafting on the Nam Khan River in Laos

Nam Suang River: Located near Luang Namtha, this river has a range of rapids ranging from Class II to Class IV. It's an excellent choice for seasoned kayakers.

Kayaking and rafting on the Nam Suang River in Laos

Nam Pa River: Located in Vang Vieng, this river has calm rapids and an excellent landscape. It's an excellent option for families and beginners.

Nam Ming River: Located in Vang Vieng, this river has a range of rapids ranging from Class II to Class IV. It's an excellent choice for seasoned kayakers.

Here are a few things to consider before going kayaking or rafting in Laos:

- The weather in Laos may be unpredictable, so check the forecast before you arrive.

- The water levels in the rivers can also fluctuate fast, so consult with your guide before embarking on your journey.
- Keep an eye out for animals in the vicinity. Laos is home to a variety of snakes and insects, so take care.
- Consider the environment. Leave no trace and avoid polluting the waters.

Kayaking and rafting in Laos are fantastic ways to enjoy the country's natural beauty while having an amazing adventure. You may have a safe and fun trip with a little forethought.

Elephant Trekking

For good reason, elephant trekking is a popular tourist activity in Laos. It's a one-of-a-kind chance to enjoy the splendor of the Laotian countryside while learning about these magnificent species.

There are several elephant trekking businesses in Laos, making it difficult to pick one. *Here are a few things to consider before making your decision:*

- Choose an ethical firm that cares about elephants. Some elephant trekking firms employ severe training methods that push elephants to perform things they do not want to do. Choose a firm that only employs positive reinforcement and enables the elephants to wander freely in their natural habitat.
- Select a firm that provides a variety of activities. Some elephant trekking organizations just provide rides, while others include a variety of other activities such as bathing, feeding, and learning about elephant behavior. Choose a firm that provides a range of activities if you want a more immersive experience.
- Choose a firm that is in a lovely location. Elephant trekking is a terrific way to view the countryside, so look for a firm that is located in a scenic region.

- You're ready to begin your journey after you've picked an elephant trekking provider! What to anticipate on a Laos elephant trekking tour:
- You'll begin by meeting the elephants and their mahouts (trainers). The mahouts will instruct you on how to interact with the elephants and how to ride them securely.
- You'll then begin your journey through the jungle. The elephants will go gently through the forest, allowing you plenty of time to enjoy the landscape.
- You could stop along the way to feed or bathe the elephants. You may also get the opportunity to learn about elephant behavior and its significance in Laotian culture.
- After a few hours of hiking, you'll arrive at a stunning waterfall. Swim in the waterfall or simply relax and soak in the sights.
- The walk will then return to the elephant camp. Before returning to your accommodation, you will get the opportunity to say your goodbyes to the elephants and mahouts.

- Elephant trekking is really a one-of-a-kind and amazing experience. If you want to connect with nature and learn about these incredible creatures, elephant trekking in Laos is the right activity for you.

Here are some more suggestions for elephant trekking in Laos:

- Dress comfortably and with shoes that allow you to move freely. You'll be doing a lot of walking, so make sure you're comfy.
- Bring sunscreen, sunglasses, and a hat. In Laos, the sun may be intense, therefore it's critical to protect oneself from the elements.
- Bring a camera to document your experiences. Your elephant trekking excursion will undoubtedly result in some spectacular photographs.
- Respect the elephants and their mahouts. Elephants are clever and sensitive creatures that must be treated with care.

Have a good time! Relax and enjoy the incredible experience of elephant trekking.

Cooking Classes

In Laos, there are many different culinary lessons to choose from, so you may pick one that suits your interests and budget. Some workshops focus on traditional Laotian foods, while others provide a more cosmopolitan menu. There are also lessons specialized to specific nutritional demands, such as vegetarian or vegan cuisine. Whatever style of culinary lesson you take, you will undoubtedly learn a lot about Laotian cuisine. You will learn about the many ingredients used in Laotian cooking, as well as the various techniques used. You will also be able to sample some delectable Laotian foods.

You will not only learn about Laotian food but will also have the opportunity to see the culture firsthand. Cooking workshops are frequently given in local homes, giving you the opportunity to meet locals and learn about their way of life.

You will also get the opportunity to purchase at local markets and observe the preparation of ingredients for Laotian meals. Taking a cooking class in Laos is an excellent opportunity to learn about the culture and food of the nation. It's also a pleasurable and fulfilling experience. If you are considering a vacation to Laos, I strongly advise you to include a culinary lesson on your agenda.

Here are some of the greatest Laos cooking classes:

Madamphasouk Vientiane Cooking lesson: This lesson is offered in Vientiane in a typical Laotian household. You'll learn how to create traditional Laotian foods including laap, khao soi, and sticky rice.

The Bamboo Experience: This is a culinary class in Luang Prabang. You will learn to prepare a range of Laotian meals as well as Thai and Vietnamese dishes. You will also be able to tour a local market and learn about the products used in Laotian cookery.

Cooking classes Tamarind: This is another culinary school in Luang Prabang.

You will learn how to prepare Laotian, Thai, and European cuisine. You will also be able to tour a local market and learn about the products used in Laotian cookery.

These are just a handful of the fantastic culinary lessons offered in Laos. If you want to learn more about Laotian cuisine, I recommend doing some research and finding a program that is perfect for you.

Here are some suggestions for selecting a culinary lesson in Laos:

- Consider your interests: If you want to learn about traditional Laotian cuisine, look for a program that concentrates on these foods. If you are more interested in learning about international food, there are several excellent possibilities.
- Consider your budget: Cooking lessons can range in price from very low to fairly high. Make a

budget before you begin your search to avoid overspending.
- Read the following reviews: Before you schedule a cooking class, make sure to check feedback from previous students. This will provide you with an idea of what to expect.
- Ask around: If you know anybody who has taken a culinary lesson in Laos, ask them for recommendations. They might be able to provide you with some useful advice.

Shopping

Here are some of the greatest shopping areas in Laos:

Vientiane Night Market: Laos' largest and most popular night market. It is centrally located in Vientiane, the capital city. Everything from souvenirs to apparel to gadgets may be found here.

Talat Sao Morning Market: Another well-known market in Vientiane. It is open from early in the morning till late in the afternoon. Fresh fruit, meats, fish, and other local products are available here.

The Luang Prabang Night Market: This is located in the UNESCO World Heritage Site of Luang Prabang. It is open late in the afternoon till late in the evening. Ock **Pop Tok Living Crafts Centre:** This is a fantastic place to acquire high-quality Laotian handicrafts. Vientiane is the location of the center.

Laos Arts & Crafts Cooperative: This is another fantastic spot to buy Laotian goods. Vientiane is the location of the cooperation.

Here are some shopping recommendations for Laos:

- Bargaining is anticipated in the majority of Laos' marketplaces. Don't be scared to bargain on pricing.
- When shopping at marketplaces, keep an eye on your surroundings. Pickpockets and fraudsters are commonplace.

- When purchasing handicrafts, ensure that they are created in Laos. Markets are rife with counterfeit products.
- Inquire about the materials used to make the handicrafts. Some handcrafted items may contain hazardous materials.
- Buy handcrafted items from local craftsmen to support local businesses.
- Shopping in Laos may be a fun way to learn about the culture and bring home some unusual gifts. Simply remember to negotiate, stay aware of your surroundings, and patronize local companies.

Here are some other things to consider when buying in Laos:

- Laos' currency is the kip. 1 USD = 10,000 kip is the approximate exchange rate.
- Most stores in Laos only take cash. There are abms in Vientiane and Luang Prabang, however, they are not always operational.

- When shopping at markets, it is a good idea to have modest money with you. This will make bargaining simpler.
- If you buy handicrafts, make sure to pack them properly so they don't get damaged on your trip.

Nightlife

Laos' nightlife is not as crazy as that of other Southeast Asian countries, but there are still plenty of venues to grab a drink and have some fun.

Here are some of the greatest venues in Laos to enjoy the nightlife:

Vientiane: Vientiane, the capital of Laos, has a thriving nightlife scene. Traditional Lao pubs to Western-style nightclubs are available to satisfy all preferences. *Vientiane's most prominent attractions include:*

Bor Pen Nyang: This renowned nightclub is recognized for its active dance floor and boisterous atmosphere.

Sala Sunset Khounta: This rooftop bar offers breathtaking views of the city and is ideal for a drink at sunset.

Cowboy Park: This bustling pub attracts both residents and visitors and is a fantastic spot to meet new people.

Luang Prabang is a UNESCO World Heritage Site noted for its picturesque ancient town and laid-back vibe. The nightlife in Luang Prabang is not as vibrant as that in Vientiane, but there are still plenty of venues to grab a drink and have a good time. *Some of the most prominent attractions in Luang Prabang are:*

Icon Klub: This famous nightclub attracts both residents and visitors and is a terrific spot to dance the night away.

Dao Fah Night Club: Known for its live music, this nightclub is a terrific spot to spend a night out with friends.

Lalaland Bar: This famous backpacker hangout provides a choice of beverages as well as live music.

Vang Vieng: This little town is known for its party scene and offers a variety of pubs and clubs. *Vang Vieng's most popular attractions include:*

Sakura Bar: Known for its tubing parties, Sakura Bar is a wonderful location to party with fellow backpackers.

Viva Pub: This popular local and tourist hangout serves a range of beverages and has live music.

Room 101: Known for its laid-back ambiance, this pub is a terrific location to unwind with friends.

Whatever your tastes are, you will find something to love in Laos' nightlife. So put on your dance shoes and prepare to have a good time!

<u>*Here are some suggestions for remaining safe while enjoying Laos' nightlife:*</u>

- Keep an eye out for your surroundings and never leave your drink unattended.
- Never take a drink from a stranger.
- If you are uncomfortable, trust your instincts and leave the situation.
- Instead of strolling alone at night, choose cabs or tuk-tuks.

By following these recommendations, you may help guarantee that your trip to Laos is both safe and pleasant.

Here are some other things to remember about Laos' nightlife:

- Laos' legal drinking age is 18 years old.
- Tipping is not expected, but it is valued in Laos.
- In Laos, the dress code for pubs and clubs is often casual.
- Laos' nightlife may be fairly economical, especially when compared to other Southeast Asian countries.

CHAPTER 6

Food and Drinks in Laos

As a visitor to Laos, you are in for a culinary adventure that will tantalize your taste buds and introduce you to a whole new world of flavors. From aromatic herbs and spices to exotic fruits and traditional cuisines, here is a list of the foods and beverages you must eat during your Laos visit.

Lao Food

Lao cuisine is a delectable and distinctive combination of flavors from the many diverse civilizations that have impacted the country over the years. Laos offers a diverse range of cuisines, from robust curries to fresh salads and exquisite sweets. Sticky rice is one of the most significant elements in Lao cuisine. Sticky rice is a glutinous, short-grain rice that adheres together when cooked. Sticky rice is frequently served with curry or other foods, but it is equally delicious on its own.

Herbs and spices are another significant component of Lao cuisine. Laotian chefs flavor their meals with herbs and spices such as lemongrass, galangal, kaffir lime leaves, turmeric, and chili peppers. These herbs and spices lend a particular flavor to Lao cuisine.

Here are some of the most popular Lao foods to try:

Larb: This is a Laotian national cuisine consisting of minced beef salad. Larb is usually cooked using ground pig or beef, as well as herbs, spices, and chili peppers. It's frequently served with sticky rice.

Tam Mak Hoong: Another famous Lao cuisine is green papaya salad. Green papaya, tomatoes, chili peppers, lime juice, and fish sauce are used to make Tam Mak Hoong. It's typically served with sticky rice or baguettes.

Mok Pa: A steamed fish dish that is frequently prepared in banana leaves. Mok Pa is cooked using catfish or carp, as well as herbs, spices, and chili peppers. It's a light and tasty dish that's ideal for a summer dinner.

Khao Piak Sen: This is a noodle soup prepared with flat rice noodles, chicken or pork, herbs, and spices. Khao Piak Sen is a tasty and substantial dish that is ideal for a cold day.

Naem Khao Tod: Crispy rice salad prepared with crispy rice, herbs, spices, and chili peppers. Naem Khao Tod is a tasty and unusual snack that is ideal for sharing.

Sausages from Laos: Lao sausages are classified into two types: sai ua and sai gok. Sai ua is a pig sausage seasoned with lemongrass, galangal, and chili peppers.

Sai gok: This is a kind of chicken sausage flavored with lemongrass, galangal, and turmeric. Both kinds of Lao sausage are great on their own or as part of a bigger meal.

Lao cuisine is a delightful and unique way to learn about Lao culture. Visitors to Laos should surely taste some of the country's numerous wonderful meals.

Here are some suggestions for enjoying Lao cuisine as a visitor:

- Be adventurous: Lao cuisine incorporates plants and spices that you may not be familiar with. Be daring and try new things. You may be surprised with what you enjoy!
- If you're not sure what to order, ask your waiter or waitress for suggestions. They would gladly assist you in finding something you will appreciate.
- Eat with your hands: It is normal to eat with your hands in Laos. This may appear unusual at first, but it's a lot of fun! Just make sure to fully wash your hands before you begin eating.
- Enjoy yourself: Lao cuisine is more than simply food. It's a way of life for them. Take in the environment and relish the experience. You will not be sorry!

Lao Drinks

Lao beverages are not only refreshing and tasty, but they also give a unique glimpse into this Southeast Asian country's rich cultural legacy. Lao beverages are a wonderful feast for the senses, ranging from scented teas to strong rice wines.

The legendary Lao coffee is one of the most recognizable Lao beverages. Laos is well-known for its high-quality coffee beans cultivated in the lush Bolaven Plateau in the country's south. Lao coffee is traditionally brewed with a traditional filter known as a **"*phin,*"** which allows the coffee to soak gently, producing a rich and delicious cup of joe. Lao coffee, whether hot or cold, is a must-try for each tourist.

Another famous Lao beverage is the pleasant and tart lime juice known as **"*nam ma nao.*"** Nam ma nao, made with freshly squeezed limes, water, and a touch of sugar, is the ideal thirst quencher on a hot day. It is frequently served over ice and topped with a sprig of mint, which adds a touch of freshness to the drink. Nam ma nao is a real Lao classic due to its blend of sweet, tart, and lemony flavors.

Lao rice wine, or **"lao-lao,"** is a must-try for anyone looking for a more adventurous drinking experience. Lao-Lao is a distilled traditional liquor derived from fermented sticky rice. It is frequently handmade and can range in intensity from moderate to quite powerful. Lao-Lao is often served in shot glasses and is a favorite option for celebratory events. Lao-Lao is not for the faint of heart, but for those who enjoy a decent drink, it provides a distinct sense of local culture.

Tea aficionados will be in heaven in Laos since the country has a vast selection of fragrant and tasty teas. **"nam dok anchan,"** or butterfly pea blossom tea, is one of the most popular. This tea, made from the vivid blue petals of the butterfly pea flower, is not only visually appealing but also has a mild and earthy flavor. It is frequently served hot or iced and can be consumed straight or sweetened with honey.

In addition to these traditional beverages, Laos is well-known for its extensive selection of fruit shakes and smoothies. Visitors may enjoy a pleasant and healthful treat with an abundance of tropical fruits such as mangoes, pineapples, and coconuts. These fruit shakes are frequently created to request, with your preferred fruit combined with ice and a dash of coconut milk or yogurt. They are the ideal way to chill down and enjoy Laos' exotic flavors.

Exploring the native beverages as a guest in Laos is not just a gastronomic adventure but also a cultural experience. Each sip conveys a tale, reflecting the country's traditions, flavors, and history. Whether you're sipping Lao coffee, drinking rice wine, or indulging in a fruit smoothie, Lao beverages will make an indelible mark on your taste buds and recollections. Raise your glass to the rich and diverse world of Lao drinks. Cheers!

Where to Eat in Laos

Laos has a diverse range of dining options, from local street food booths to sophisticated dining establishments. *Here are a couple of my suggestions:*

Lao Kitchen: This Vientiane restaurant provides authentic Lao food in a relaxed atmosphere. The menu includes foods such as laap (minced pork salad), tam mak hoong (green papaya salad), and khao piak sen (wet rice noodles).

Kualao: This Vientiane fine dining restaurant provides a contemporary perspective on Lao food. Grilled wagyu beef with black pepper sauce and stir-fried river snails with lemongrass and chilies are among the foods on the menu.

Lao Home Cook: In Luang Prabang, this family-run restaurant provides genuine Lao food in a cozy atmosphere. Mok pa (steamed fish wrapped in banana leaves) and sai gok (grilled pork sausage) are among the delicacies on the menu.

The Boathouse: Located on the Mekong River in Luang Prabang, this restaurant provides spectacular views of the river and surrounding landscape. The menu includes a selection of foreign meals as well as Lao favorites.

Lao BBQ: This Luang Prabang street food cart is a terrific spot to taste grilled meats and fish. Grilled chicken, hog, and beef, as well as grilled fish and shrimp, are on the menu.

In addition to these eateries, Laos has a plethora of additional excellent dining options. *Here are some pointers for discovering tasty food:*

- Look for eateries that are crowded with locals. This is a positive sign if the meal is tasty and real.
- Request suggestions from your accommodation or tour guide. They will be able to recommend some of the greatest restaurants in the neighborhood.
- Be daring and try new dishes. Lao food is rich with delectable and distinct flavors.

You will discover wonderful meals no matter where you go in Laos. So savor your dinner and the flavors of this lovely nation.

Here are some more dining recommendations for Laos:

- Sticky rice is a staple delicacy in Laos and is eaten with nearly every meal. It is produced from glutinous rice that has been cooked till mushy and sticky. Sticky rice may be consumed on its own or used to scoop up other foods.
- Laap: Laap is a Laotian national cuisine consisting of minced pork salad. Ground meat (typically pig or beef), fresh herbs, chiles, and lime juice are used to make it. Laap can be eaten on its own or alongside sticky rice.
- Tam mak hoong (green papaya salad): Tam mak hoong is a famous meal in Laos. It's made of shredded green papaya, tomatoes, chiles, lime juice, and fish sauce. Tam mak hoong is a light and refreshing salad that is ideal for a hot day.

- Khao piak sen: Khao piak sen is a popular wet rice noodle soup in Laos. Rice noodles, chicken or beef broth, fresh herbs, and chiles are used to make this dish. Khao piak sen is a warming and filling soup that is ideal for a cold day.

CHAPTER 7

Tips for Traveling in Laos

Exploring Laos as a guest may be a rewarding experience. Here are some crucial recommendations to bear in mind while traveling in Laos to make the most of your vacation.

Be Prepared for the Heat and Humidity

The heat and humidity are two things that tourists to Laos should be prepared for. Laos' average temperature is 28 degrees Celsius (82 degrees Fahrenheit), and humidity levels may be quite high, particularly during the rainy season. This can be quite unpleasant, and it is critical to take precautions to remain cool and hydrated.

Here are some suggestions for remaining cool and hydrated when visiting Laos:

- Wear light-colored, loose-fitting clothes. This will allow your body to cool down more quickly.
- Wearing synthetic textiles is not recommended since they trap heat and moisture.
- Consume lots of fluids, particularly water. Drink at least eight glasses of water each day.
- Avoid drinking alcohol and caffeine, which might dehydrate you.
- Bathe or shower in chilly water.
- Stay as much as possible in the shade.
- Take pauses from activities during the day.
- Seek medical treatment if you are feeling ill.

<u>Here are some more safety considerations for dealing with heat and humidity:</u>

- Recognize the symptoms of heat exhaustion and heatstroke. Heat exhaustion is a minor kind of heart disease that can result in headaches, dizziness, nausea, and muscular cramps. Heatstroke is a more severe and potentially lethal condition. If you see any of these symptoms, get medical care right away.

- Never leave children or pets in a hot car unattended.
- When exercising in hot temperatures, use caution. Begin cautiously and progressively raise your activity level.
- If you intend to spend time outside, bring sunscreen, a hat, and sunglasses.

By following these guidelines, you may help to guarantee that your vacation to Laos is safe and enjoyable, even in the heat and humidity.

Here are some other things to think about when preparing for the heat and humidity in Laos:

- If you're coming from a colder climate, bring a couple of additional layers of clothes. The temperature can drop dramatically at night, particularly in the highlands.

- Make sure to bring bug repellant. Mosquitoes may be a nuisance in Laos, particularly during the rainy season.
- If you intend to go hiking or trekking, make sure to have proper footwear and gear. The terrain in Laos may be difficult, and it is critical to be prepared for all weather situations.
- Before traveling to Laos, learn about the local customs and etiquette. This will assist you in avoiding any cultural faux pas.

You can easily prepare for the heat and humidity in Laos with a little forethought and have a safe and happy vacation.

Learn Some Basic Lao Phrases

Here are some of the most useful Lao phrases for visitors:

Greetings:

- Sai-bai-dee (ສະບາຍດ) - Hello
- Jao sai-bai-dee baw? (ຈາ ສະບາຍດ ບ ?) - How are you?
- Sai-bai-dee (ສະບາຍດ) - I'm fine
- Sabai dee ka (ສະບາຍດ ຂ້າ) - Hello (female)
- Sabai dee kha (ສະບາຍດ ຂ້າ) - Hello (male)
- Polite phrases:
- Khâw thôht (ຂ ໂທດ) - Excuse me
- Kalouna (ຂ ລອນ) - Please
- Khop jai (ຂອບໃຈ) - Thank you
- Khop jai lai lai (ຂອບໃຈ ລາຍ ລາຍ) - Thank you very much
- Baw pen niang (ບ ເປັນຫຍັງ) - You're welcome

Essential phrases:

- Do you speak English? - Khon thoe English bo? (ຂອບໃຈ ທ ານ ເວ້າ ອັງກດ ບ ?)
- Where is the bathroom? - Hawng nam yuu sai? (ຫ້ອງນ້ຳ ຢູ່ ໃສ?)

- How much does this cost? - Laka tao dai? (ລາຄາ ເທົ່າໃດ?)
- I would like to buy this. - Khoy yark khao ni. (ຂ້ອຍ ຢາກ ຊື້ ນີ້.)
- I am lost. - Khoy tee hai. (ຂ້ອຍ ເສຍຫາຍ.)

These are just a handful of the numerous helpful Lao words you might learn. You will have a more pleasurable and rewarding journey to Laos if you take the time to learn a few words.

Here are some more pointers for learning Lao phrases:

- Begin with the fundamentals. Learn the most often used greetings, polite phrases, and key phrases.
- Practice on a regular basis. The more you practice, the better your Lao will get.
- Make no apologies about making blunders. When learning a new language, everyone makes mistakes.

- Please be patient. Learning a new language takes time. Don't get disheartened if you don't learn Lao overnight.
- Learning a few basic Lao words can allow you to converse with the people and enhance your vacation to Laos. So, what are you holding out for? Begin learning right

Bargain When Shopping

Bargaining is a popular practice in Laos, and visitors are encouraged to negotiate when purchasing at marketplaces and businesses. <u>Here are some pointers on how to properly bargain in Laos:</u>

- Do your homework. Before you begin haggling, it is useful to know the approximate worth of the object you wish to purchase. This will assist you in avoiding being overcharged. You may conduct research by asking other travelers, reading guidebooks, or looking up prices online.

- Begin slowly. When you initially begin haggling, offer a price that is far lower than the asking amount. This will offer you some wiggle room while negotiating. For example, if the asking price is 100,000 kip, you may begin by making an offer of 50,000 kip.
- Be self-assured. It is critical to be confident while bargaining. The vendor will be less willing to negotiate with you if you appear uncertain or unsure of yourself.
- Please be patient. Bargaining can be time-consuming, so be patient. Don't be disappointed if the vendor rejects your initial offer. Simply keep haggling until you find an arrangement that you both agree on.
- Be nice and smile. Even when bargaining, it is crucial to be courteous and respectful to the vendor. This will contribute to a more favorable environment and make the bargaining process more fun.
- Don't be frightened to leave. If you are dissatisfied with the seller's offer, do not be afraid

to walk away. The identical item may be found in a variety of other shops and marketplaces around Laos.

Here are some more negotiation techniques for Laos:

- To communicate with the merchant, use gestures and body language.
- If you are not satisfied with the price, be prepared to walk away.
- If you're having trouble bargaining, don't be embarrassed to seek assistance from a local.
- Bargaining may be a joyful and pleasurable element of Laos shopping. By following these suggestions, you may receive the best deals on souvenirs and other items.

Here are some of the greatest bargaining spots in Laos:

Vientiane's main market, Talat Sao Market, is an excellent destination to get souvenirs, handicrafts, and apparel.

Luang Prabang Morning Market: Held every morning, this market is a terrific location to purchase fresh food, local cuisines, and gifts.

Nong Khai Night Market: This market is in Nong Khai, which is located directly across the Mekong River from Thailand. It is an excellent location for purchasing souvenirs, apparel, and gadgets.

Van Vieng Night Market: This market is located in the renowned tourist area of Vang Vieng. It is an excellent location for purchasing souvenirs, clothes, and cuisine.

Talay Taeng Market: This market is located approximately an hour's drive from Luang Prabang in the town of Talay Taeng. It is an excellent location for purchasing hill tribal goods and souvenirs.

It is critical to be respectful and polite when dealing with Laos. Remember that the vendor is only trying to make a buck, so don't be too pushy. You'll be negotiating like a pro in no time if you practice!

Be Respectful of Local Culture

Laos is a lovely nation with a fascinating culture and history. Visitors visiting Laos are frequently struck by the Lao people's friendliness and kindness. When visiting Laos, however, it is essential to respect the local culture. *Here are some pointers on how to go about it:*

- Learn some fundamental Lao phrases. Even a few words, such as "hello," "goodbye," "thank you," and "please," will demonstrate that you are attempting to connect with the locals.
- Wear something modest. It is vital to dress modestly when visiting temples or other sacred locations. Covering your shoulders and knees is required.
- Before entering a temple or a residence, take off your shoes. In Laos, this is a gesture of respect.
- Be aware of your body language. It is considered impolite to point with your feet. Avoid establishing direct eye contact with seniors as

well, since this might be perceived as disrespectful.
- Keep an eye on your surroundings. Laos is a secure nation, but you should constantly be alert of your surroundings and take measures against petty theft.
- Be environmentally conscious. Laos is a lovely nation with a delicate environment. Please contribute to environmental protection by properly disposing of rubbish and avoiding littering.

By following these suggestions, you can help to guarantee that your trip to Laos is enjoyable for both you and the natives.

Here are some more suggestions for respecting Laotian culture:

- Do not criticize the monarchy or the government. Laos is a communist country where leaders are held in high regard. It is critical to refrain from

criticizing the government or the monarchy, as this may insult local sensitivities.
- Be mindful of cultural taboos. In Laos, there are certain cultural taboos, such as pointing with your feet, touching a monk, or eating in front of a Buddha picture. It is essential to be aware of these taboos and refrain from doing anything that may offend local sensitivities.
- Demonstrate your enthusiasm for Lao culture. Learning about and appreciating local culture is one of the finest ways to demonstrate respect for it. Visit museums and cultural centers, sample Lao cuisine, and learn a few Lao languages. You will demonstrate your respect for the Lao people by exhibiting an interest in Lao culture.

By following these guidelines, you may assist in ensuring that your trip to Laos is both courteous and enjoyable for all parties involved.

Tipping is not expected in Laos

Tipping is not expected as a visitor in Laos. In fact, it is frequently seen as impolite or even unpleasant. This is due to the fact that tipping is not a part of Lao culture. Lao people feel that everyone should be given a living salary and that tipping is unnecessary. This rule does have a few exceptions. A service fee may be added to the bill at some high-end restaurants and hotels. It is typical in this situation to round up the bill to the closest dollar. If you had a very nice experience, you may choose to tip your guide or driver.

Here are some tipping guidelines for Laos:

- You are not required to tip. Tipping is not expected, and failing to tip is not considered impolite.
- Be discreet if you wish to tip. Tipping in front of other people might be considered humiliating.

- The tip should be kept to a minimum. A few thousand kips (the native money) is more than plenty.
- Tipping is not required for taxi, tuk-tuk, or motorcycle drivers. You can negotiate the fare ahead of time, and you are not required to tip for good service.
- Tipping is not permitted at temples or religious buildings. Tipping is considered impolite at some establishments.
- If you are unclear about whether to tip, it is usually advisable to err on the side of caution and refrain from tipping. Tipping is not customary in Laos, thus it is better to be safe than sorry.

<u>Here are some alternative methods to express your gratitude for exceptional service in Laos:</u>

- Thank you with a smile. A simple grin and thank you may go a long way toward expressing your gratitude.

- Give a modest token of your appreciation. A simple present, such as a box of chocolates or a bottle of wine, is a nice way to express your gratitude.
- Write a favorable review. A favorable TripAdvisor or other travel website review can help support local businesses while also encouraging other travelers to visit Laos.

You may show your appreciation for good service in Laos without tipping if you follow these suggestions.

Cultural etiquette in Laos

The following are some of the most significant cultural etiquette standards to remember when visiting Laos:

- Wear something modest. It is vital to dress modestly when visiting temples or holy locations. Covering your shoulders and knees is required. In

general, dress cautiously in Laos, since exposing apparel may be considered rude.
- When entering a temple or a private residence, remove your shoes. This is a respectful gesture.
- Do not point your foot at people or icons of Buddha. In Laos, the feet are considered filthy, hence pointing your feet at someone or a Buddha picture is considered insulting.
- Do not approach a monk. Women should avoid touching monks in particular. Touching a monk's robes or body is deemed rude.
- Take no pictures of individuals without their consent. This is considered impolite in Laos.
- Take note of your noise levels. Because Laos is a rather peaceful nation, it is critical to be cautious of your noise levels. In public situations, avoid screaming or making loud noises.
- Respect your elders. Elders are regarded in great regard in Laos, thus it is critical to respect them. This includes using courteous words and avoiding impolite gestures.

- Please be patient. Laos has a significantly slower pace of life than many Western countries. Be patient while waiting for things to happen, and don't become irritated if things don't go as planned.
- Learn some fundamental Lao phrases. This will demonstrate to the Lao people that you are interested in learning about their culture.
- Keep an open mind and be courteous. Laos is a lovely nation with a fascinating culture. Maintain an open mind and respect for the Lao people and their way of life.

You may have a courteous and pleasurable vacation to Laos if you observe these cultural etiquette norms.

<u>Here are some extra suggestions for Laos visitors:</u>

- Discover Lao culture. Take some time to study about Lao culture before visiting Laos. This will assist you in understanding ethnic etiquette standards and avoiding faux pas.

- Prepare yourself for the heat. Laos is a hot nation, so dress accordingly. Wear light-colored, loose-fitting clothes and drink lots of water.
- Keep an eye out for landmines. Laos still has landmines, so be aware of the dangers and take measures. Avoid going off the main route and exercise caution whether hiking or bicycling.
- Help the local economy. Try to support the local economy while in Laos by dining at local restaurants, buying at local markets, and employing local guides.
- Make no traces. When visiting Laos, be cautious to leave no trace. This includes taking away your trash and being environmentally conscious.

By following these guidelines, you may guarantee that your trip to Laos is safe, polite, and enjoyable.

Emergency Contacts

For travelers, below is a list of emergency contacts in Laos:

- 1191, 241162, 241163, 241164, and 212703 police officers
- Tourist Police Number: 021-251-128
- Fire: 1190
- 1195 (Ambulance)
- 1199 kWh of electricity
- Water: 1198
- Gas: 1197
- 1623 or 1624 Roadside Assistance
- 1192 lost and found items
- 1193 Visas and Immigration
- 1194 Foreign Embassies

These numbers should be kept on your phone or written down in case of an emergency. These numbers can also be found on the website of your embassy or consulate in Laos.

In addition to these emergency numbers, there are a few additional key people to call when in Laos:

Medical Services: A number of hospitals and clinics in Laos provide medical services to international visitors. For urgent medical crises, the Vientiane International **Hospital:** This is a viable choice. You can also go to a neighborhood clinic or drugstore for less critical medical requirements.

Diplomatic Missions: Laos has a number of diplomatic missions that can aid foreigners in an emergency. Vientiane is home to the Australian Embassy, the British Embassy, and the Canadian Embassy.

If you are traveling with a tour operator, they should be able to offer you emergency help if necessary.

When visiting any nation, it is always a good idea to be prepared for an emergency. By saving the emergency contacts for Laos in your phone or writing them down, you may ensure that you will be able to obtain the assistance you require in the event of an emergency.

Here are some more safety recommendations for Laos:

- Maintain vigilance and take safeguards against petty theft.
- Do not consume tap water.
- Crossing the street should be done with caution because traffic regulations are not usually obeyed.
- Understand the dangers of malaria and other tropical illnesses.
- Before you leave, purchase travel insurance.

You may assist in guaranteeing a safe and pleasurable vacation to Laos by following these guidelines.

Conclusion

In the concluding chapter of this book on Laos, we find ourselves reflecting on the rich tapestry of history, culture, and natural beauty that this enchanting country has to offer. As we say goodbye to the pages that have unfolded in front of us, we are left with a tremendous sense of amazement and respect for Laos' grandeur.

The ending is a touching reminder of the Lao people's tenacity and spirit since they have faced several obstacles throughout their history. It is a monument to their persistent commitment to maintain their distinct heritage and customs in the face of the nation's changing winds. Furthermore, the ending emphasizes the great natural beauty that blesses Laos' surroundings. This area is a treasure mine of spectacular vistas and experiences, from the beautiful Mekong River to the lush forests and mist-covered mountains.

The book's conclusion asks readers to immerse themselves in Laos' tranquility, discover its hidden treasures, and appreciate the delicate balance between human existence and the natural world.

Finally, we are left with a sense of desire and curiosity, prompting us to go on our own adventure to Laos. It is an invitation to uncover unknown stories, embrace the warmth of the Lao people, and be charmed by this amazing country's eternal attraction.

Safe Vacation!

Travel Planner

Memories From My Laos Trip

Date: _____ Destination: _____

NOTE

_____
_____
_____
_____
_____
_____
_____
_____
_____
_____
_____
_____

Memories From My Laos Trip

Date: _____ Destination: _____

NOTE

Memories From My Laos Trip

Date: _____ Destination: _____

NOTE

_____
_____
_____
_____
_____
_____
_____
_____
_____
_____
_____

Memories From My Laos Trip

Date: _____ Destination: _____

NOTE

_____
_____
_____
_____
_____
_____
_____
_____
_____
_____
_____

Memories From My Laos Trip

Date: _____ Destination: _____

NOTE

_____
_____
_____
_____
_____
_____
_____
_____
_____
_____
_____

Memories From My Laos Trip

Date: _____ Destination: _____

NOTE

_____
_____
_____
_____
_____
_____
_____
_____
_____
_____
_____

Memories From My Laos Trip

Date: _____ Destination: _____

NOTE

Memories From My Laos Trip

Date: _____ Destination: _____

NOTE

_____
_____
_____
_____
_____
_____
_____
_____
_____
_____
_____
_____

Memories From My Laos Trip

Date: _____ Destination: _____

NOTE

Memories From My Laos Trip

Date: _____ Destination: _____

NOTE

_____
_____
_____
_____
_____
_____
_____
_____
_____
_____
_____
_____

Memories From My Laos Trip

Date: Destination:

NOTE

Memories From My Laos Trip

Date: _____ Destination: _____

NOTE

_____
_____
_____
_____
_____
_____
_____
_____
_____
_____
_____
_____

Memories From My Laos Trip

Date: _____ Destination: _____

NOTE

_____
_____
_____
_____
_____
_____
_____
_____
_____
_____
_____

Memories From My Laos Trip

Date: _____ Destination: _____

NOTE

_____
_____
_____
_____
_____
_____
_____
_____
_____
_____
_____
_____

Memories From My Laos Trip

Date:　　　　　　　　　　Destination:

NOTE

Memories From My Laos Trip

Date: Destination:

NOTE

Printed in Great Britain
by Amazon